THE
HUSBAND

AARON DANIEL BEHR

Columbus Press
P.O. Box 91028
Columbus, OH 43209
www.ColumbusPressBooks.com

EDITORS
Brad Pauquette and Emily Hitchcock

ARTWORK, DESIGN & PRODUCTION
Columbus Publishing Lab
www.ColumbusPublishingLab.com

E-book: 978-1-63337-185-9
Paperback: 978-1-63337-186-6
Hardback: 978-1-63337-187-3

Printed in the United States of America
1 3 5 7 9 10 8 6 4 2

This book is dedicated to Dan and Coralee Behr. They believed in me when no one else would and have never stopped loving me.

My brothers Andrew, Adam, Dillon Sprague who have all, at times, carried the mantle of Superhero in my life.

To God, He'll never leave nor forsake me. He'll always love and cherish me. He's victorious yesterday, today, and tomorrow.

Editor's Note

What you are about to read is based on actual events, recounted through the lens of the author's memory.

This narrative is of course biased, flawed, broken, incomplete, imperfect. The author is a human being.

We live in a world of competing perspectives. Broken, flawed, biased perspectives. In so many cases, the truth is hidden in the confluence of these voices.

In divorce, the husband's voice is most likely to be omitted. A man is 39% more likely to commit suicide after a divorce than a woman. Our support systems and cultural values are largely skewed to support women through a divorce.

If we are to address the divorce epidemic, we need to hear all of the voices. We need to challenge our stereotypes of abuse and victimization. The Husband brings a new perspective to the table, and provides invaluable insight into the plight of the forsaken man.

PART ONE
THE BREAKING POINT

April 8, 2017 – Friday

The Husband stands at a sturdy 6'2", weighs 220 pounds, squats twice his bodyweight, benches over 350 pounds, has a broad muscular physique, and a heavy brow. He's smart. Not anything prizeworthy, but averagely good enough that he can, on special occasions, seem more intellectual than he is. He is thirty-four years old. He chooses baldness over thinning hair.

At this moment in The Husband's long and trial-filled life, he flips his hoodie over his head, shoves his hands into his pockets, and marches down a sparsely lit parking lot. At the end is his tiny black sedan. It's nearly six years old, but on just the right night, still has that brand-new-car smell. He climbs inside and takes a deep breath.

Alone on a Friday, he decided to drive an hour to Columbus to watch a late showing of a depressing movie, and now it is one in the morning. His thoughts are consumed by his wife, The Wife. Worry, like bugs, slowly begins to crawl on his skin.

As The Husband sits quietly inside his chilly car, he grips the wheel and fights back ruminations. He knows The Wife is close to her coworker, The Coworker, and is with him on a work trip that began Wednesday. He knows they have been texting outside of work about subjects unrelated to the job. However, The Wife continues to reassure The Husband that she and The Coworker are accompanied by their boss, The Boss. That and her relationship with The Coworker is harmless, like a brother and sister relationship.

The Husband cannot shake this uneasy feeling from his racing thoughts. He went through something akin to this with The Ex in his first marriage. It reminds him of when The Ex would go to conferences, only to meet up with the man who would later be The Ex's new husband. But The Wife would never do something like that. He loves The Wife and she loves him.

The Husband picks up his phone and unlocks it. Its low light is the only thing that illuminates the small front seat. The Wife's last message is generic. Not a "goodnight" or a "take care." It holds only a general and insincere concern, like all her messages as of late. Nerves and an intensely beating heart tell The Husband to dial her. Tonight is her last night. She will be on the road the next day and two other men will be there to drive. There is no reason why she can't talk now.

Many years ago, before she became The Wife, she would stay up talking to him as he returned from work in Columbus. It is an hour drive so there's no reason why she wouldn't now. The Husband acts on his compulsion and dials. There's no answer. He leaves a message. She calls him in the middle of the message. He tries to express himself from behind a foreboding fear.

The Wife whispers, "Hello?"

"Hey." He doesn't know what to say. There's a heavy weight on his chest and shoulders. It's hard to breathe and talk. He decides to start driving, fidget, and get moving so he can talk. "How are you?"

"Sleeping." Still in a whisper she continues, "Are you OK?"

"Yeah, I um…" He tries to talk with the phone to his ear as he shifts his manual car. "I went to a movie."

"That's good."

Both are silent for a moment.

He holds the phone on his shoulder then manages the standard transmission as he enters the highway. "It was good. How was your night?"

"Good…but…I need to go."

"Why?" Third gear shifts into fourth.

She whispers, "I've got to leave tomorrow."

"But you aren't driving."

"I know…but I just need to get some rest."

"Sleep in the car on the way there." The Husband tries to sound confident but his countenance won't allow him. "You can keep me awake."

She sighs. "I'm too tired."

"I know but it'll be like when we were dating." He shifts into fifth and his poor car roars as it desperately tries to travel 70 mph. "Talk me home."

Her whispers become frustrated. "I really need to go."

"Why? I need to talk. I'm struggling with some things."

"We can talk tomorrow."

Tears build in The Husband's eyes. The center yellow lines blur with headlight beams and black asphalt. "Why are you trying to get rid of me?"

Again, she sighs. "I'm not... I'm tired."

"You've barely told me anything about your week."

The Wife's whisper is barely audible, "Tomorrow."

"Why are you whispering?"

"I'm tired."

His throat is bottlenecked by a lump preventing words from leaving his mouth. "Is someone there?"

"No. I need to get some sleep."

"I need your help."

The Wife is clearly annoyed. "Goodbye...I need to sleep."

"Why? Why are you trying to get rid of me?" He starts to openly sob. "I'm your husband, why are you pushing me off the phone." His mind screams at him that there is a man with her. That she is cheating, and it is The Coworker.

He does his best to quiet those thoughts. This is The Wife. This is the beauty that he loves with his entire person, all his being. To him she is the greatest thing on the earth. She is kind and good. She is smart and caring. She knows what he went through, the pain, the trauma he suffered under The Ex. He sacrificed so much for The Wife—rebuilt a home with her, took whatever job came along to make ends meet—he will do anything for her.

This is The Wife, the "in sickness and health, till death do us part" wife. The Ex was a fluke. This one is for real. She loves God. She loves The Husband. This is his workout buddy, The Wife for whom he cooks nearly every meal, The Wife for whom he put his own dreams on hold, so she could find her dream. This is The Wife who just got her perfect job after years of crying on his shoulder, leaning on him for support through career move after career move until she made it.

There is no way she is having an affair...

August 2011

The failed first marriage had The Husband feeling like a loser. He ignored it and began the harrowing task of rebuilding his life. The church he started attending had a weekend leadership enrichment retreat. The first full day, The Husband noticed an adorable girl with a heart-shaped face. She was wearing the only pair of trouser jeans left in the world, a baggy long-sleeve Ohio State shirt, and her brown hair was parted down the middle.

Honestly, she wasn't The Husband's type. She was short, way too skinny, and made no efforts to look beautiful. That fact strangely attracted him to her. Despite all the thrift store clothing, the 60s hair tucked behind tiny ears, and no makeup, she was gorgeous. He couldn't stop staring at her.

There was a sunrise in her smile, one that reminded him it's a new day with new hopes. Her eyes and her entire face were filled with happiness. She had an intoxicating laugh. The harder she laughed, the more she'd snort. It shook her entire body. It was authentic.

The retreat attendees played a game inside the pole barn sanctuary. There was a line of masking tape down the center of an old brown outdoor carpet. The game was simple. Its purpose was a "getting to know you" exercise. Everyone stood on the line. The Husband found himself at the front.

Someone called out, "Step right if you're a dog person. Step left if you're a cat person."

The Husband stepped left, turned around, and caught The Girl's sunrise smile. Her eyes boldly met his. He felt himself returning the cheesiest grin. It sent tingling warmth through his veins as if she were his boyhood crush.

They all stepped into the center. The same person called, "Right for Pepsi. Left for Coke."

The Husband stepped left, turned around, and there was The Girl. She bore the same overwhelming smile. Back to the center, they called out something else, and both The Husband and The Girl stepped right.

Their steps moved together more than not. When lunch rolled around, he knew he had to sit at her table and he did, directly across from her.

Each person introduced themselves as they shoveled cold-cut sandwiches into their mouths. It didn't take long before The Girl's attention was firmly glued to The Husband, and his to her.

He asked, "So tell me what you do?"

"I work at the Naz as sort of a donor." She did this cute contorting of her eyebrows and continued, "It's really handing out scholarships and asking for donors. How about you?"

He looked down at his barely eaten sandwich and poked it. "I work at a department store but it's temporary. I'm looking for something better. I've got a bachelor's in English and communication from the Naz, which means my options for work are a little limited." He chuckled. "What's your degree in?"

"I have a BS in social work and my master's in social work administration."

"You already have your master's? Congrats."

"Thanks." She blushed.

At twenty-eight, he had to figure out if she was within age range to be a viable candidate. He tried to do the math, which was one of his weaknesses. She probably went to college at eighteen, four years in undergraduate school, two for the master's, and she spent a year working at MVNU. She had to be about twenty-five. That wasn't bad. "I was working on my master's in English, but I really want to be a writer."

"Yeah?" She leaned forward. "What've you written?"

"Fiction, novels." He scooted closer to the edge of his metal folding chair. "I've written three."

"Wow!" Honest interest was plastered on her face.

They went on to talk their lunch away and found as many moments as possible to hover near each other during the conference. It didn't matter that his mad genius math was skewed and she was actually only twenty-one. The Husband left on a high. It didn't matter that he had to drive an hour for work or that his manager was an even bigger jerk that evening.

The next day they sat next to one another in church and chatted. He could barely pay attention to the service. In one moment they all had their hands raised, in that cheerful "God scored a touchdown" sort of way. The Husband looked over to The Girl and thought to himself, *I want to be with this girl.*

Afterward, because he was deathly afraid to ask a girl like her out, he did something casual. "So, I um…" He picked at a hole in his jeans. "Was wondering, this movie came out that I want to see. You could join me for dinner and we could keep it simple."

Her face sunk. "I um…I've sort of been talking to someone else." She started picking at the ends of her fingers. "I'm sorry."

"No, it's OK…"

It wasn't. In two days of interacting and a friend request online, she never once mentioned being in a relationship. He tried to laugh it off, but it nagged at him. That thought, that word: *Loser.*

A Long Time before April 8, 2017

The Husband began as The Boy who grew up in the small town of Mount Vernon, Ohio. He was the eldest of three brothers. His father was a professor working a dream job, and his mother was a college grad working to make ends meet. They attended church every Sunday morning and night as well as Wednesday evenings.

For The Boy, school was...difficult. He was constantly bullied, which led to fist fights. Every night and morning he fought an emotional battle to convince himself to go to school. He was sad, cried often, and feared being at school as well as church.

In the early nineties, school districts were handing out Ritalin like candy. Every child who had any behavioral problems was diagnosed with ADHD. To the authorities in The Boy's life, this was the answer to all his behavioral problems.

A psychologist determined that The Boy had a generalized anxiety disorder. They quickly put him on Buspar, patted him on the bum, and sent him back into the world. It worked, for a time, but The Boy was still depressed.

The psychiatrist's answer was to put The Boy on Prozac. By the fourth grade The Boy became The Zombie. He would shuffle into school, zone out into outer space, and shuffle back home. Friendless, he'd spend his evenings in his room with Legos or his favorite hobby, staring at a nice corner of the bedroom ceiling.

The Boy, now The Zombie, was still being bullied, but like a good zombie he stood and drooled as this happened. The teachers eventually saw this and took sympathy on him. Instead of letting The Zombie go out to recess, they sat him in a small cabinet with a book.

High on Buspar and Prozac, The Zombie was sure of one thing— there was something wrong with him. He was not normal. He'd sit in class and think that he would always be nothing, a loser. Up to this point, that's how he was treated, and the medication made him feel like nothing, dead. He was yearning for death.

◆ ◆ ◆

By the end of fifth grade The Zombie wanted to be a boy again; he wanted to be normal. He stopped taking the pills. As his system detoxed he was in the most paranoid and aggressive state of his life. Within the first week of being off the meds, he found himself in the bathroom with two other boys.

It was one of those boys' restrooms that always smelled like fresh hot urine. The endless lines of grout between tiny blue squares of tile had turned brown and black from years of boys missing their target. A row of sinks ran parallel to three urinals and three toilets.

White tiles with gold and silver sprinkles covered half the wall, and ugly teal filled the rest. The ceilings were high. They were covered in some material that looked like white cotton if someone had thrown dirt at it. On the farthest wall was a noisy heater with a frosted window behind it.

The Boy finished his business, zipped up his pants, and stepped out of the toilet stall. Two boys stood waiting for him as if it were some cliché eighties film. One was shorter than the other.

The Short One taunted, "You're in the wrong restroom. The girls' is across the hall."

The Tall One thumbed in that direction.

The Boy lowered his head and pushed by them. His already ringing ears felt like they were on fire. The fast beating of his heart, which kept him from sleeping the night before, only picked up speed. He turned on the water and washed his hands.

Before he could finish, they were in his space.

The Tall One said to the shorter, "He's such a retard."

"I'm not a retard." Anger swelled inside of The Boy. He sharply jerked his chin up and to the left a couple of times.

"Oh no?" The Shorter One flattened his palm and wildly slammed his thumb into his chest. "Duh…you act retarded to me…duh…"

Red surrounded The Boy's vision. Not a thought passed his mind, and before he knew it, he had balled his right hand into a fist and whirled in one powerful motion. Knuckles met the center of The Short One's face. That stopped his chest thumping.

The Short One screamed and grabbed his nose. He backed away from The Boy and kept wailing. The Tall One wound up his fist like he saw all the wrestlers on television do, but The Boy was quick. Someone started yelling from a distance.

Years of soccer gave him fast reflexes and a powerful right leg. He swung his foot toward the inside ankle of The Tall One's right leg. Foot met leg before The Tall One's fist had finished winding.

The Tall One did an awkward split and fell to his back with his right leg bent in an unnatural direction. The ring of his head hitting the blue tiles had barely sounded before The Boy drove his fist toward The Tall One's face.

The Tall One moved in time to take the blow to the side of his head. His body went slack. The yelling in the distance grew louder.

The Boy readied to return to The Short One before he finally registered the yell, "Stop! Stop it now!" The stentorian voice repeated The Boy's name along with those three words repeatedly.

It finally registered with The Boy. He stepped back from the two lying at his feet. The Tall One blinked his eyes to life. The Short One sat on the floor, rocking back and forth. Blood poured between the fingers covering his face.

The Boy finally made eye contact with the distant voice. It was his teacher, one of three male teachers at the school. He was a few feet away and flushed. The edge of his lips quivered, which twitched his nose. Tall and imposing, he had his arms spread out and his fists were ready to leap.

Everything that had happened flashed in replay in The Boy's mind.

It bashed him with dizziness. He thumped his palms into the sides of his head and began to shake it. Tears ran down his face. "I'm sorry… I didn't mean to… They called me a retard… They called me a girl."

The teacher angrily screamed at The Boy, "It doesn't matter!"

"I felt like…like…"

He couldn't articulate it at the time, but it was powerlessness, over himself, over the boys, as if he had no control over his actions.

The Principal had no choice but to expel The "Unwell" Zombie. The Mom and The Dad responded by choosing to never let The Boy return. They homeschooled him. The Mom eventually quit her soul-sucking job to teach all three of her boys full time. This was a financial blow to the family.

Often The Dad would ask him, "What were you thinking?"

"I don't know."

Then The Boy would grab the sides of his head and shake it. He was sure of one thing, he was a loser.

April 9, 2017 – Early Saturday

The Husband arrives at home around two in the morning. Yellow house lights combine with the streetlamp to illuminate the home clear as day. It has charcoal grey siding, purple shutters, and a matching plum-colored front door, which they painted together.

He wipes away the tears that he cried while he begged The Wife to stay on the line. The empty house greets him as coldly as The Wife remains. He shoulders the phone and opens the door. "What time are you leaving tomorrow?" He closes the heavy front door behind him, latches it, and walks down the narrow passage created by the back of the dirt-brown couch to his right and an antique dresser to his left.

"Checkout is eleven."

"Why not sooner?" He turns on the lamp on top of the dresser, and moves to the hallway where he flips a switch to break the darkness. "You've got nothing going on tomorrow."

"I don't know." She drops back to a whisper, "Our boss is slow in the mornings."

The Husband's insecurities ask again, "So your boss and coworker are sharing a room?"

"Yeah...are you home yet?"

"I'm home." The bedroom light on the nightstand is already glowing. He starts stripping down to his underwear. "Please stay with me until I climb into bed."

"I need to get some sleep!" She sounds exasperated.

He pulls himself into the queen-size bed. The bedside lamp makes it too bright to sleep, but at this moment, the vastness of the empty bed only seems safe with her beside him or illuminated. He says, "In bed."

"OK...get some sleep."

"I'll try...you too... Thanks for staying on the line. I love you."

She says, "I miss you too," but it is quiet and insincere. The phone beeps as she ends the call.

The Husband sets the phone underneath his chin. He stares at the bright bulb on top of the table. Tears pool in his eyes. This year he has hated himself and it has affected The Wife. He is sure of this. He knows he hasn't been good at managing his anxieties and depression. He has let the pressure to make money, to be someone, rule him.

Every failure from a lost job, every turned down application fuels memories of the bullies and his teachers. They echo insults from the past. It's as if his mind escapes for a moment into a room with a tall bookshelf. He pulls open a book and flips through pages of pictures with decorative captions. The pictures show all the bullies in his past and the captions are the insults they hurled at him.

The light of his phone clicks back on and his heart skips. There's no message. He reaches for the lamp, turns it off. The glow of the phone lasts a minute and then it's black. The hall light radiates into the room a little. In that moment, The Husband wishes for nothing more than The Wife to be in his arms. In that moment, he formulates a plan to get everything back on track.

They'll work this out, they have in the past. He is going to do everything in his power to make sure. He begs God for help, for strength, for change, for forgiveness, for everything he can think of, and then the morning sun washes into the room. He takes a deep breath and can smell her perfume in the empty bed next to him.

Somewhere around November 2016

The Husband learned he had a toxic goiter in his right thyroid. The doctor told him he had hyperthyroidism. Surgery was the best option. The thought terrified him.

Working as a substitute teacher and unable to find a job that wouldn't suck out his soul, there was pressure building in his household for him to make money. Holiday break was around the corner, which meant days he wasn't going to get paid.

It was a Saturday. The Husband was feeling particularly low. He ambled into the living room. Several burning candles smelled like cinnamon. The Wife was sitting on the couch that, along with the antique dresser, bottlenecked the foyer. The front bay windows beside the couch filled the room with heat and sunlight.

With her elbows on her knees, she turned her head to face him. There was no glow to her that day. Her hair was pulled back by a headband. She somberly said, "We're living outside of our budget."

"What? I've been working nearly every day." It was draining. Every day he stepped into the high school or middle school was another reminder that he had accomplished nothing with his life. He stopped writing, which was a calling God had given him at a young age. The only reason he worked out was because she did. "What do you want me to do?"

She shrugged and flopped back against the couch. "I don't know." She started picking at the skin at the ends of her fingers.

"I've been applying for jobs."

"I've been applying for jobs for you." She turned her gaze up to him.

"What? Do you want me to work at a factory, second and third shifts like I did all throughout college?"

"No…" She returned her attention to her fingers. "You just need to apply yourself a little better."

"OK." The Husband's shoulders sagged. "I mean, every job I apply for barely pays minimum wage. I don't have the education you have. There's nothing impressive about my resume. I mean…" He rubbed his forehead. "If you expected me to be the breadwinner, I won't ever be, not in this town."

"I'm not asking you to be the breadwinner." She stopped picking and leaned forward over the laptop on the coffee table. "I can move some things around. It's just…"

"What?"

She looked up at him; there was a cold indifference in her countenance. "My parents are very traditional. They expect you to be making money. That's not what I expect."

"I can't." He slouched then flipped over his palms as if he were asking for forgiveness. "I'm the worst I've ever been. I need help."

She sighed. "What kind of help?"

"I don't know." His hand returned to his forehead. "I need a pill or something. I just want to shut the thinking off so I can get up and do these soul-sucking jobs. Maybe I should find a therapist."

She shrugged. "Maybe."

"Look…I need help. I hate my life. I don't know what the answer is anymore. I've worked sixty hours a week on minimum wage. You get to work your dream. I want the same. I can't take another pointless job just for the paycheck."

The Wife stared at him blankly, cold again. "Do whatever you want." She grabbed her phone and started thumbing it. "You know, when you say you hate your life, you're saying that you hate me."

"No, that's not what I'm saying at all." He changed the tone of his voice to be more comforting and said, "I'm just saying I feel horrible. It's not about you. It's just…I hate this town…there're no opportunities for me."

"It's not all about you. You hurt my feelings when you say you hate your life."

The Husband walked closer and she was quick to tuck her phone under her thigh. He sat next to her. "I love you. Believe me, there's no one I ever want to be married to but you."

"I know." She flopped back. "I love you too."

"I'll um…" He rubbed his throat. The lump hurt when he was the most stressed. "I'll find a therapist. I don't want to have to start taking meds. And then we can text our friend and see who she suggests as a surgeon in Columbus."

"I'll text her. I can help find the surgeon."

"Thank you."

The next day, The Husband found a therapist. When it came to the surgery, they talked about it and The Wife decided that it would be best to wait until his parents returned from the Philippines. He was unsure about this decision.

In the meantime, The Wife learned that she had precancerous spots on her cervix. The Husband's surgery was put aside indefinitely because The Wife's was more important and they "couldn't afford both." The Wife's surgery shook The Husband to his core. Just thinking about it threw him into panic over her safety.

Fast Forward to April 8, 2017 – Saturday

The Husband climbs out of bed, showers, and cleans the house. He throws the sheets in the laundry, does a couple loads, folds them, and puts them in the proper place. Around the middle of the day he runs to the store to get her favorite meal: sirloin steak, salad, and sweet potatoes. Somewhere around one, he receives a text from The Wife that reads, "We're stopping for lunch. It'll be an hour."

The Husband does the math. The hotel is about four hours away. If they waited until the last minute to leave, eleven, stopped an hour or two for lunch, a rough estimate would put them in town at five or six. He replies, "Tell me when you get close and I'll make dinner. Are you dropping your boss off first?" She was riding in The Coworker's car.

Her reply, "Yeah, he's on the way home."

Around five o'clock he asks her if she is close. Her reply is short and devoid of character, like each of her replies her entire trip. "No."

He tries to chat with her, but she takes forever to respond. This week she claimed to be too busy, today she claims she is getting carsick.

After seven she sends him a text that she is thirty minutes away, so he throws everything together. He bakes the potatoes into fries, grills the steaks, makes the salad, sets the table, and uncorks her favorite wine. His heart has been racing all day.

At seven-forty-five, The Coworker's SUV rolls into the driveway. The Husband watches from the front window as The Coworker helps her get her suitcase from the trunk. They linger back there for a bit. Then they round the vehicle, side by side, smiling, glowing, and share a long goodbye.

Again, The Husband must fight the feelings of betrayal. Not The Wife. She would never do that to him. She knows that would devastate him. He swings open the door and gives her a gleeful welcome. The glow she showed her coworker turns to a blank stare.

The Husband takes her bags and says, "Dinner's ready. Did you have a good drive?" He reaches for a hug.

"It's OK." She breezes past him. "We had a big lunch."

He follows. "You got your boss dropped off?"

"Mhmm." From the other room, she says, "This looks good."

The Husband is sleep deprived. His heart is beating out of his chest. All his fears seem to rest in his legs. It's like trudging through mud to walk from the living room to the dining room. He takes his seat next to her at the end of the brand new high-top table.

The dining room is small. Images of wine bottles adorn the room. A sign hangs behind her. It reads, "God, bless this house."

They try to eat but neither seems to have an appetite. She asks about his day. He tells her everything he did. She doesn't seem to care. The Husband says, "I think we need to talk. I know I've been real depressed lately and I've had an anxious week, but I feel like something's going on between us and we should work on it."

She shifts uncomfortably in her seat. "Yeah we need to talk."

Her tone causes him to stare at his half-eaten steak. "What's been going on?"

Simply, matter-of-factly, she says, "I want a divorce."

The Husband wants to run. He can hardly believe his ears. That panic he felt while she was in her surgery, the dizziness he felt when surrounded by bullies, and that feeling of being powerless dumps into his head. He begins to openly cry as he asks, "Why?"

The Wife then gives him a litany of reasons. He has lost his drive, his depression and anxieties are too much and abusive, there isn't enough money, he's not attentive to her needs, his unhappiness has worn her down, the house isn't clean enough, he's not applying himself to find a job.

He openly weeps and shakes. "I'm sorry. Why all of this? Why now? We can fix it. I can be better. I'm already going to therapy. This doesn't make any sense. There's no need to have a divorce."

"I'm just not happy anymore." Her stare is trite. "I just can't make you happy. I've tried, and I can't do anything."

He begs, "That's my fault. I'm so sorry. Please forgive me. We can work on this."

"No, we can't. We aren't good for each other. We've both been unhappy our entire marriage."

Full body, gut wrenching sobs pour out of The Husband. "That's not true. I love you more than the day I met you. There has to be something else going on, there has to be another man. There is, isn't there?" The Ex had given him the same speech—down to the exact "happiness" phrase—before he learned of her affair.

The Wife shakes her head. It is condescending. "No. There's no one else. We just aren't good for each other."

He tries to argue with her, plead with her to no avail. She repeats, "It's over and there's nothing you can say or do to convince me otherwise." He cleans the kitchen as he listens and argues with her about her list of reasons.

They get ready for bed, turn out the lights, and The Husband tries his best to muffle his crying. He prays to God, "Please don't let this be happening. Please fix this. Kill me. I can't take this pain." Every so often he breaks down and openly wails. She half-heartedly tries to comfort him. He continues to pray and sob until the sun rises.

Fall 2011

The Girl stopped "talking" to the other guy and became The Girlfriend. She was amazing. They could talk for hours. Laughter was always a staple of the time they spent together. She was completely different than any girl he had ever been with. It was as if she was meant to be in his arms.

A huge part of him felt like she was a gift from God. He wasn't in the kind of crazy euphoric love that had landed him in the center of a courthouse with The Ex. This was dramatically different. There was a portion of wise-mindedness to his emotions that told him this was right. He prayed about it constantly.

One cold day, they both went to a Christian music festival in town. They mostly hung on each other. Somehow, this loser was able to live in the moment. He just enjoyed every minute with her.

When they climbed into the tiny black sedan they cranked up the heat and tried to get warm. Its brand-new-car smell filled the air.

"You know what I want?" asked The Husband. "Are you in the mood for tomato soup with grilled cheese sandwiches?"

"Yeah!" She beamed.

The house she was sitting for that week was all white, from the walls to tightly-woven carpet that smelled like hot plastic. The kitchen had a brown tint to it but was lightly colored. It was a "U" shape with a breakfast bar and stools on one side.

The Husband started the soups. She was by his side. She rested her elbows on the counter, her chin in her palms, and talked to him. He didn't mind doing the work, he loved it.

When the meal was cooked, they sat side-by-side at the breakfast bar. She tore off a crust of bread and dipped it into the soup. The Husband was still chilly, so he plunged his spoon into the warm soup. He made a loud slurp.

"Are you slurping your soup?" She had a twinkle of ornery about her.

"Yes, ma'am." He filled his spoon, leaned close to the soup, and slurped as loudly as he could. "It tastes better if you slurp it."

She laughed hard enough to snort. When she caught her breath, she lifted a spoon to her lips, and looked up with determination as if he had dared her to do it.

"Trust me," he said.

She took a long loud slurp then nearly choked with laughter. He echoed her. That moment froze in his mind. He found one of the only good scrapbooks from his mental bookshelf and dropped it in with the caption, "Slurping makes soup taste better."

She leaned in and kissed him. To him, it was perfect. Suddenly the rest of his bookshelf full of proof that he was a loser no longer mattered. He was of value to this stunningly brilliant girl. A girl he never felt he deserved.

He opened his eyes and captured her expression. The sincerity of it made him woozy. This was their first kiss, and strangely it felt like the first of his life. Then, as quickly as it happened, she pulled back and set her soup onto the counter. She said, "I umm... I started something didn't I?"

"I think so." He put his soup down, wrapped his hand behind her head, and pulled her in for a kiss. It was longer, even more beautiful than the last.

He kept his hand behind her head and his forehead on hers. She looked up at him. They locked gazes, and somehow the closeness didn't blur the image of her gorgeous brown eyes. "I've wanted to do that all night," he said.

"Me too." She lifted her mouth back to his.

April 9, 2017 – Sunday

The Husband sets to work making The Wife's day as perfect as possible. He is assertive, plans a day of shopping in Columbus and going to their favorite winery. She is agreeable but still distant.

With little to no sleep, he is running completely on adrenaline and fear. She wants to leave for Columbus later in the day, but at noon she comes to him and without looking says, "I think I'm going to go to the grocery and do some shopping before we leave."

"Cool." The Husband smiles brightly. "I can go with you."

"No..." She pauses. "I just need to clear my head." Now she looks him in the eyes and gives him a half smile. "You play some games and I'll be back in a little bit."

His heart begins to beat faster. "OK...you're sure you don't want me to go with you?"

"I'm sure." She leaves the room, shuffles around the house a bit, and then says, "Bye," as she closes the front door behind her.

He plays games in "his" room. Here he has a futon, a dresser for his clothing, a small closet, and a desk for his gaming computer. He tries not to worry about the time. It's early enough for his dad to still be online. Both The Mom and The Dad are part-time missionaries to the Philippines. They already know about The Wife's intention for a divorce. The Dad tells the son, "Well, do whatever it takes to make it right to your wife. Work on things."

An hour passes without a word from her. His heart is beating so hard it is building pressure in his ears, like when a plane lands. He texts The Dad, who is twelve hours ahead, "I know it's insane, but I feel like she's having an affair."

The Dad replies, "That's insane. Your wife would never do that. Make sure you remain cool and calm and respectful. Trust in God."

Then another hour passes. He checks his phone often but there's nothing. Finally, two and a half hours later, the front door opens, and she shuffles into the house. She yells, "I'm home."

From the other room he yells back, "How'd it go? Do you need help unloading the car?" He climbs out of his chair to greet her.

She ghosts past him, keeps her head down, and replies, "No," followed by a forced laugh. "I only got a few things. My head was just in space the entire time. I literally stood in the aisles staring blankly at things."

He follows her into the kitchen. "What all did you get?"

Another feigned chuckle and she replies, "Just a few things." One by one, she pulls out the contents of a plastic bag, six items in all.

"Two and a half hours and that's it?" They are things they don't even need. "Well, are you ready to head to Columbus?" He holds out his arms for a hug.

She returns his embrace with a rushed half-hearted hug. "Yeah, let me change."

They travel to Columbus. He plays music they listened to while dating. The conversation is light and upbeat. She tells him about the evening activities she went to on her trip—piano bars, pubs, maybe a dance place, he can hardly pay attention.

She makes jokes about The Boss's interaction with her and The Coworker. How she and The Coworker told these little inside jokes, but The Boss's hearing was poor. They knew he laughed because he saw them laughing, and not because of what they were saying.

The date begins at a winery in a Columbus shopping plaza. Inside, there are two long marble bars with a matching circular one in the middle of the room. Racks of wine line the walls. Tables displaying wine decorations, decanters and breakables fill most of the empty space. It feels claustrophobic on a slow day.

It's a crowded afternoon but they find a spot at the center counter. The Husband doesn't feel like doing this today. He's nauseous. Jitters from lack of sleep twitch his muscles. He braces himself on the side of the cold counter with both hands.

The Wife spent most of the car ride focusing on her phone and continues the habit. The Husband does his best to keep this from bothering him, but his heart continues to thump.

The waiter is a tall friendly gentleman. A couple of old ladies are flirting with him. Finally, he breaks away from their attention and turns to The Husband and Wife's table. Gleefully, he asks, "Will you be having the tasting of the month or a sweet tasting today?"

In near unison, they reply, "The month's."

"That's easy enough." He pulls tiny square napkins from underneath the counter and places one in front of each of them. Then he fishes out two glasses and sets them on the napkins. He begins with a description of the first wine, then pours them each a little.

Their conversation flutters around different subjects as they drink the first glass and move to the next. She continues to keep her phone close to her side, but the alcohol is taking the edge off The Husband's anxieties.

By the fourth glass they are giggling. Somehow the subject of talk lands on silly songs they used to sing as kids. The Wife pulls up a song. The room is noisy and the speakers on her phone aren't that great, but he bends low so they can put it up to their ears. They sing along to a song about a hairbrush, a cheeseburger, and pirates. They laugh together.

Something about this moment slows time for The Husband. There's an eerie feeling to it. Whether it's the drinks, the exhaustion, or something else, his mind returns again and again to the thought, *This is The Girl who used to slurp soup with me.*

After a while The Wife heads to the bathroom and disappears there for longer than usual. For a brief second, his knees buckle. He nearly topples to the ground but braces himself again against the coolness of the marble countertop.

The Wife returns. She's finishing a text as she approaches the counter. He tries to capture how beautiful she is. She's wearing a tight-fitting red top with his favorite jeans.

Dinner, conversation, a walk around the open mall, and then they are back in the car heading home by seven. She is texting. Her phone shifts between blue text and green as she exchanges long messages.

The Husband watches this out of the corner of his eye and suspicion grows. He sees The Wife receive a large block of text and finally he asks, "Who are you talking to?"

She replies with the name of a friend.

This answer doesn't sit well with The Husband. He asks to see the messages.

She opens her last conversation with the friend. It isn't the same conversation he was just watching. The messages coming in seconds earlier were paragraphs long, while the conversation she displays for him now contains only short sentences and GIFs. He confronts her. "That's not the text I saw a second ago. Don't lie to me. Who are you talking to?"

The Wife begins shifting in her seat as if she's sitting on something uncomfortable. She bobs the phone between her hands. Then she rests her head on the back of the seat, and turns to him so that he gets a strong whiff of the perfume he bought her for their honeymoon. It's a choco-laty floral scent. She whispers, "My coworker."

The Husband's heart explodes. The largest headache he's ever had hits him. His vision skips the red foggy stage of his childhood and blurs to near blackout. His thought processing shuts off as he asks, "Are you having an affair with him?"

Again, she hesitates. "Yes."

Fall 2011

The Husband stood in his parents' kitchen, the far edge of an open-lay-out ranch home. The ceilings were vaulted; the counters formed an "L" with a sink in front of a bar on the farthest end. Beyond the bar sat a small breakfast table with a family room on one side and white French doors on the other. Sunlight oppressively filled the long room.

Trouble consumed The Husband. It clutched his thoughts as he rinsed dishes in the porcelain sink and slid them into the dishwasher next to him. The counters were a dark green, near black, with grey marbling. They showed every speck of sugar or flour. He began to wipe them down as The Mom walked into the room.

There was something beautiful about The Mom's appearance. She had aged incredibly well, dyeing her hair the dark blonde color of her youth, and staying conscientious of current women's styles as she grew older.

She had always been a guiding light to his emotional self. She understood how he was feeling at any given time. They were alike in how overwhelming their emotions could become, and this mutual understanding bonded their relationship further.

He must have sighed because she asked, "What's the matter?"

"Me?" He continued to vigorously attack some sticky spot left behind from dinner. "Nothing."

"Nothing?"

He returned to the sink and rinsed the rag. His mother rounded the bar to face him from the other side. "I can tell."

"I don't know what to do." He squeezed the rag tight.

"About?"

"Everything." He hung the rag on the center of the sink divider. "The Girl."

"What about her?"

He braced himself on the edge of the counter. "I love her. We're even talking about marriage. I just don't know." He rubbed his forehead and instantly regretted it because his hands were still wet.

The Mother crossed her arms and rested her elbows on the counter. "What don't you know?"

"I don't know if I should." He used his hand to make gestures as he talked. "I've already failed at one marriage. The Ex made everyone I care about choose sides. I nearly lost all my friends from high school and college, namely The Bud. Here I am in my parents' basement rebuilding a life I lost."

"So? That's life. Maybe God is giving you a second chance. Maybe He gave you this girl because you've always wanted to be a husband."

He pressed his palms to the side of his head and then released them. "I just don't know. There are things about her that bother me."

"Like what?"

"I don't know."

"Red flags?"

"I mean…" He thought about it for a minute. "Not really. She's smart, beautiful; her parents seem like sane Christians. She's completely different from my ex. She cares about me. She goes out of her way to show her love to me. I feel reaffirmed. I just don't know if I can trust her. I'd die if she did what my ex did."

"Listen, I didn't get involved when you and your first wife ran to the courthouse. But I'm going to tell you, when a girl as kind, loyal, and loving as this girl wants to marry you, you'd be a fool not to trust her."

The Husband sighed then braced himself against the sink again. His mother was right.

The Ex was self-centered. All she cared about was herself. He knew that. He had always known that, but for some reason she had loved him. He felt that all marriages were work, no matter if he married the perfect person or grew with an imperfect person.

That night he began ring shopping. It made his heart flutter. There was something about it that terrified him. A small, still voice told him not to do it. He ignored it and prayed. Assurance filled him. This was the right thing to do.

April 9, 2017 – Sunday

The minute The Wife confirms an affair, warm tingling climbs The Husband's spine, a fog settles on his vision, and he begins losing control. He shakes, sobbing, dizzy, and can't sit still. He begins a barrage of questions. "So Friday night, Saturday morning, he was in bed with you?"

She drops her head. "Yes."

His heart stops. That moment freezes. The night before rapidly replays in his head. He asks, "What did your boss say about the two of you sharing a room?"

"My boss didn't go." The car swerves. "Maybe you should pull over."

It's as if The Husband has been punched in the face. To him, there is no longer a road. He is blinded by the cloud growing in his brain. He asks, "Did you spend all three nights in the same room?"

"Yes."

The wind is audibly knocked out of him. "Why'd your boss allow you two to get a room together?"

"He didn't... We charged the organization for two hotel rooms."

The Husband tries to put all the pieces together. "So, all those stories about your nights out were actually about your dates with him?"

She finally looks up at him. "Yes...you should really pull over and let me drive." She grips the side of the door. "What do you want me to say?"

"So yesterday, as I was doing everything in my power to build a plan to keep us together, and I impatiently waited—looked forward to your arrival—you spent a long morning in bed with him and took your time coming home?"

"What do you want me to say?"

"Answer the question!"

"Yes."

He can't ask another word. There's not enough room in his brain. He is shaking.

She begs, "Please stop the car, pull over, let me drive."

"No..." He tries to remain calm, tries to breathe, but the weight on his chest is too heavy. Somehow, they make it home. He mad-dashes into the house, drops his keys, picks up his phone and calls his parents. He doesn't even know who has answered when he screams, "She's having an affair!" He's pacing wildly around the family room.

The Parents are on speakerphone, each trying to calm him down. He is panicking. The Wife saunters into the house. She's texting someone.

The Husband hangs up with his parents, grabs his keys, and heads for the door.

She steps in the way. "Wait...where are you going?"

"I need to get out of here."

"Don't do anything stupid."

He sternly tells her, "Move."

She does, and he sprints to the car. His body is trembling so much that he can barely find the key to unlock the door. Somehow, he does, climbs inside, starts the car, and wildly peels out of the driveway. His phone rings. It's The Dad. He answers.

The Dad and Mom tell him to calm down, that they are with him. The relationship isn't over yet, and it can still be salvaged. Somehow, they talk sense into his storm-filled head.

When the fog lifts, he finds himself at a red light a few miles from home. He doesn't know where he's going. He turns back around and drives home. He walks inside, and The Wife is talking on her phone. Calmly, but with an edge of anger in his voice, he asks, "Who are you talking to?"

"I'm telling him what's going on."

"Give it to me." The Husband holds out his hand.

"What are you going to say?"

The Husband shakes his head. "Give me the phone or I'll call him myself. I'll get right back into that car and go to his front steps if I have to."

She warns The Coworker then hands the phone to The Husband.

The Husband says, "You piece of—don't screw over my marriage because you've ruined your own! For once in your pathetic little life be a man. Tell your wife what you've done."

The Coworker's wormy voice replies, "Wait, this isn't all my fault. Your wife—"

"She was being a self-centered monster just like you. I'm dealing with her."

"Then I deserve the right to deal with my wife the way I want."

The Husband glares at The Wife. Her shoulders are shrugged forward, her face is downcast, and he can't tell if she is ashamed or angry. "Fine. But I'm warning you, don't take long. You don't want me to have the power to tell her myself."

"Judging by everything your wife has told me, and how you're acting now, you deserve all of this."

The Husband growls, "Really? And what'd your wife do to deserve this?"

The line is silent. The Husband hangs up the phone and returns it to The Wife. He begins pacing from the living room, through the dining room, to the kitchen. Pictures of them as a happy couple adorn the shelves and walls. They burn his heart. He can't believe she did this. Not her, she was the one, THE ONE! She would never do this to him. Not her. She treated the marriage, all they sacrificed, all they built, like dirt.

Without another thought he begins grabbing pictures of them together—her with that sunrise smile—off the walls and shelves, and slams them into the wooden floor of the living room. "This is what you've done to us, to our marriage. You've treated it like it means nothing! You've destroyed it!"

She starts bawling, the most authentic emotion she's shown in three days. She begs him to stop, that they are glass, but there's no point. She didn't stop before she let The Coworker wrap his arms around her at night.

The haze lifts and every picture lays in a pile of glass and broken frames in the center of the room. He realizes he's breathing hard and tries to control it. The Wife steps into the mess. She's sobbing.

"You can…" He runs his hand over his stubble-haired head. "You can clean this up. I'm going to go lie down…cool down." She fetches a broom and dust pan from the hallway closet.

The Husband climbs into the queen-size bed. He sharply twists his chin into the air and drops his body onto the pillow. He lightly traces his jawline with his knuckle, and drags it from ear to chin. Then he does it again. His body is worn-out and tired.

In this moment, he feels like that boy again: the one with two bullies on the floor in the boys' restroom. All the guilt and shame of years of acting out of control wash over him. He unconsciously pulls the scrapbook from his mental shelf. It contains every fight, every condescending word spoken by church members, teachers, principals, all his elders. He slams his knuckle into his jaw and drags it to his chin.

The weight of it all rests heavy on his shoulders and chest. He wants to run, get into the car, drive all the way to Texas, and step onto that brown dead ground. He wants to walk into the giant blue sky, to keep walking, to get as close to the spectacle of the setting sun over the desert of West Texas. Purples, pinks, oranges, a perfectly choreographed show.

The noise of glass being swept into a dust pan penetrates the thin wooden door of his room. He ignores it, shuts his eyes, and turns out the light.

After a while of open sobbing and cleaning, The Wife quietly slides into the bed next to him. They lay there, with a gulf of blankets between them. She meekly asks, "What do you want me to do?"

He lays with his back to her. "You cleaned up the glass?"

"Yes."

"The pictures?"

"Only a few were ruined."

"OK." He clenches his jaw. "Thank you for cleaning it up."

"I told my parents."

He tries not to reply but she doesn't offer any more details. "And?"

"They're disappointed but say they are advocating for us."

"Good."

She asks, "Do you want me to leave…stay the night at my parents' house?"

The streetlight outside their window is the only thing illuminating the room. It reminds him of the day before, the empty bed, the aching over her absence. "No. I don't want to spend another night without you near me."

"OK."

"Will you go to my therapy session with me tomorrow?"

"I have to work."

"Please."

It takes her a while before she hesitantly nuzzles next to him. "I'll go."

December 10, 2011

They were at a wedding reception in a country lodge. The room was a massive open space with vaulted ceilings and gorgeous wood trimming throughout. It was decorated in sparkling silver snowflakes with blue and white Christmas trees.

A giant two-way wood burning fireplace stood on the opposite side of the entrance. The wedding party lined a long table in front of it. Blue and silver stockings hung on the mantel. They bore the names of the wedding party.

The Girl sat among the bridesmaids. She looked stunning. Her hair was pulled back and she was wearing an ankle-length blue dress. It was strapless. The past few months of lifting weights with The Husband had filled out her shoulders, back, and arms. She beamed that sunrise smile.

The Husband was a stranger, seated with the misfit attendees—the handful of people who knew the bride or groom and no one else. They weren't a boring group, but The Husband was more interested in getting to dance with The Girl.

For a moment, a white flutter pulled his focus from The Girl. On both sides of the fireplace were glass double doors to the outdoors. Giant snowflakes fell onto the already snow-covered countryside. An impulsive decision churned inside of The Husband as he watched this perfect scene.

He sprung from his seat and out through the front doors. As he did, he caught the eye of The Girl, but he disappeared into the cold before he could sign a message. Bowing his head and wrapping himself in his arms, he trudged through the snow to his salt-caked sedan. His black and white Chucks did very little to keep his feet warm.

Shivering, he climbed into the car. The new-car smell mixed with the smell of burning wood and snowfall. He popped open the glove box, took a deep breath, and plunged in his hand. He shuffled papers around until he found what he was looking for and pulled it to his lap.

It was a small black ring box that had faded with age. He popped it open and inside was the wedding ring he had bought nearly six weeks earlier. It was silver, with a large diamond in the center. The band had a slight wave to it akin to the center line of a yin-yang symbol. The band he left at home had a row of smaller diamonds that locked into the wave. It was tightly sandwiched in the silk supports of the box. This was the box The Mom's wedding ring was in when The Dad proposed.

In that moment, with the cold billowing into his car along with the sweet scent of firewood, he could hardly believe what he was doing. A part of him felt stupid for proposing during another person's wedding, but it was the perfect setting. The snow, the Christmas trees. The DJ was even playing classic Rat Pack music. The Girl had said she wanted a December proposal, and he lived to give her whatever she wanted.

A small still voice told him not to follow through with it, but it was promptly ignored. He closed the box and shoved it in his pocket. Then he marched through the snow and back inside the lodge. The Girl's stare, from across the room, met him. She held up her hands in a shrug as if to ask, "Where did you go?"

The Husband smiled and waved. He found his seat with the misfits and tried to calm himself by taking deep breaths. His leg wouldn't stop bobbing.

The DJ changed the music and the entire wedding party had some choreographed dance they had to do. It felt like it went on forever. Finally, the first song for everyone to participate in was one of those group dances with special moves. The Husband sprang up, prayed the box wouldn't bulge too much in his pocket, and took his place at The Girl's side.

He had to watch her arms and footwork to mimic the moves. They were happy. It was the most fun he had ever had with a girl. The next song was another they could dance to and both did, wildly.

After a few songs, The Girl said, "I'm going to sit down for a bit and take a break."

"Wait." He was sweating all over the place. "Come outside with me a second, please. I just need a minute to cool down."

She looked at the falling snow and then back at The Husband. "It's too cold out there for this dress. We spent our entire time taking pictures out there. I'm just now warming up."

"Please." The Husband pouted like a puppy dog. "You can stand next to the fire."

"OK." She was hesitant. They both moved through the crowd of dancers toward the double doors on the right. He held the door open and she said, "Thank you," then promptly cried, "oh my gosh! It's freaking cold out here!"

They walked onto a patio underneath an overhang, which was protecting summer iron furniture. He led her to the double-sided fireplace where she sat down on an edging and wrapped her arms around herself.

The Husband paced for a moment. He had rehearsed this conversation, this proposal, for weeks. Adrenaline pumped through his body. He felt dizzy. Then he turned to the sunrise smile of The Girl and somehow the anxious fog lifted. He shoved his hand in his pocket, retrieved the box, and then knelt in front of her.

"You're one of the most..." He started to weep.

She matched his tears.

The entire speech vanished from his mind. All he could say was, "I love you. Please be my wife."

She excitedly said, "Yes."

They both shook as he tried to remove the ring from the box and then put it on her finger. It made them giggle even though they were crying. The ring finally slid perfectly into place.

She shivered. "It's beautiful. The curve is like the center of the yin and yang. That's us." Her teeth chattered as she leaned forward for a kiss.

At that moment, Frank Sinatra was singing from a loudspeaker inside the lodge, "Someday, when I'm awfully low, when the world is cold, I will feel a glow just thinking about you…and the way you look tonight."

April 10, 2017 – Monday

They travel to Columbus for the counseling session. On the way there, she admits that she hasn't been coming home at lunch so that she can spend more time with The Coworker. That he's been over to the house when The Husband wasn't there. This sends The Husband into a new storm.

The red blurs fill his vision. As he's gotten older, when these moments happen, he shuts down his mind. He just disappears into his thoughts. Occasionally it leads to yelling, but when it comes to The Wife, he's worked so hard to prevent that kind of response. The few times he failed haunt him.

A fit of tears falls out of him. His breathing is panicked. It's all more than he can handle. He remembers the overnight trip he took with The Bestie. He asks, "Did he come over while I was in Niagara?"

"You shouldn't be asking this while driving."

He grips the wheel tighter and pushes back the red blurs. "Did he?"

"Yes." Out of the corner of his eye, he catches her bow her head.

"Did he spend the night?"

"No, we just sat on the couch and made out."

How can he know if she is being completely honest? She hid an affair for months, maybe longer. When he asked her about it, she lied to him with a straight face. Then he pictures his living room. The couch faces a wood-burning fireplace, 1940s sandstone work, and a one-piece stone mantel. Along the top are pictures of their wedding, flowers she carried down the aisle, and a sign that reads, "And they lived happily ever after." He tilts his chin sharply up to the left.

The car swerves.

"Please let me drive."

He can't take it anymore. He yells, "No! You've put me through hell these past three days. You've literally done everything my ex did to me, play for play, word for word." His tears turn to open wailing.

The Wife's phone rings. She is quick to answer it. "Hello."

Stunned that she is taking a phone call, The Husband asks, "Who is it?"

She whispers, "Him."

"Are you freaking kidding me?!" The red invades nearly every corner of his vision. He can't control his tone. "What's wrong with you?! I'm here bawling my eyes out and you take a call from him!"

She shields the phone with her hand so she can hear The Coworker. Then she hangs up and begins texting.

"I can't believe you."

"I'm sorry. It was the work phone number. I didn't know if it was my boss or coworker."

"Then who are you texting."

She snarls, "Him."

Sternly, with a biting edge of anger, he demands, "Give me the phone."

"No." She sits back as far away from him as possible and cradles the phone to her heart.

"Give it to me."

"I'm not giving you my phone."

"Fine, tell him that we'll be done here at noon and then we're heading to The Foundation to tell your boss what you two have done. How you stole money from The Foundation to have an affair—"

"You can't."

"I will. Unless he resigns by noon, I'll tell your boss everything."

The rest of the drive to the counselor is a blur. When they get to the parking lot of the old two-story house transformed into a counseling center, he demands the phone again. "I don't know your code. I can't access it."

"Let me finish this reply." Her eyes are red and her lips pout.

He jumps out of the car. As they walk across the freshly sealed black asphalt the smell of its tar makes him gag. She stays in tow. He is fuming and continues to shake his head in disbelief.

They go through the building's birch-tree-themed entrance. The narrow foyer greets them with the staircase to the upstairs and a bathroom at the end of the hall. To their left, a living room has been repurposed into a waiting room. If there are people in there, The Husband doesn't notice. He steps into the room and begins pacing.

Water wells in The Wife's eyes. "I have to use the restroom."

"Give me your phone. I won't do anything with it. Promise." He is calmer now that he can move around.

"It doesn't matter." Her chin quivers. "He said that he and I were nothing, just a fling. That he has told his wife and just wants to work it out with her. He just wants us to forget this ever happened. He doesn't want anything to harm his or his wife's reputation." The phone is still glowing as she passes it to him.

He catches a tiny bit of the screen before she locks it. They've been talking across an email chat program to hide their tracks. When she returns, The Therapist calls them into her room.

They each take a seat on opposite sides of a grey couch. The Therapist has a short crop of black hair and sits across from them. Her eyes are wide, and she scans The Wife. The Therapist props a spiral ring notebook on her lap and asks, "What's going on?"

The Husband exclaims, "She's having an affair with her coworker."

The Wife is the angriest he has ever known her to be. She reminds him of Gollum from *The Lord of the Rings*, freaking out about a missing ring. She throws out attacks that are five years old, as if she's kept track of every misdeed he has done only to weaponize it later.

The Therapist sinks into her chair as The Husband tries to defend himself the best he can. They take turns attacking each other.

When both calm down, the Therapist leans onto her elbows and asks The Husband, "Is it OK if I share with her some of the things we've been working on?"

The Husband shrugs and says, "Sure."

"Everything you've said, everything you've both said, we've been working on, and I think he'll agree we've made a lot of progress." The Therapist elongates her neck to match eye level with The Wife. "Your husband has an attachment disorder. All those years of bullying, his parents, were magnified by the chemical reactions of his anxiety disorder. The things he is working on take years to overcome and heal from. That's why he has acted impulsively at times."

The Wife crosses her arms and clenches her teeth. They both listen to The Therapist's lecture, which finishes with, "None of this excuses your husband; it just explains why he's acted this way and I believe…" She looks to The Husband and continues, "That he's done very well and made a lot of progress."

They leave equally angry at each other. When they are back inside the car, he holds out her phone. "Call him."

"What are you going to say?" She hesitantly accepts it.

"I'm calm now. I'm just going to make it clear that he needs to resign."

"OK, let me warn him first." She dials The Coworker. There's an answer, and The Wife says, "He wants to talk to you. Uh huh. Yeah. OK. Here he is." She passes the phone back to The Husband.

The minute the phone hits his ear, The Coworker begins to yell, "You jackass! Who do you think you are? If you think you can threaten me and make me resign, you're as retarded as your wife says you are. You selfish arrogant piece of—"

The Husband yells, "Stop there!" Then he drops to a stern voice. "You've backed an angry dog into a corner. You've taken away the most valuable person in my entire life."

"Don't you blame this all on me," replies The Coworker. "You're the jackass who treats his wife horribly!"

"I love my wife. I live every day for her. Don't you dare lecture me on being a horrible husband. You're the one who cheated on your wife. You're the selfish jerk here, not me." The Husband slams his fist into his jaw. "What'd your wife do to deserve how you've treated her?"

The Coworker curses under his breath, then says, "My relationship with my wife is none of your business."

"And my relationship with my wife is none of yours." The Husband thuds his jawline again. "Look, we're an hour away from your work. I'm planning on marching into that office and demanding your resignation. That gives you until one to do what is right."

"No, that's not your right."

"I don't give a crap."

The Coworker growls, "I've got to talk to my wife first."

"I'd suggest you do it now."

"I'm going to and then I'll let you know." The Coworker stammers, "Please...please think of how this'll affect my wife. She doesn't deserve to be hurt."

The Husband laughs. "Why didn't you think about your wife before you slept with mine!"

"OK...OK..." The Coworker concedes, "I'll let you know." Then he curses under his breath.

"Good...thank you..." The Husband drops the phone in The Wife's lap.

They sit quietly for nearly the entire drive home. At one point, The Wife checks her phone and sadly proclaims, "He put in his resignation."

"Good." He tells her, "I hope you know I'm doing this for us, our family, to protect your dream. You've worked too hard to lose this job."

The car pulls into the driveway. There's a contrast that he has always loved about the house. It's a charcoal grey with the door of the one-car garage painted pure white. He remembers installing it. The roof shingles are black. The Wife, Father-In-Law, and The Husband spent the hottest day of the summer putting those on the roof. They installed cute plum shutters and painted the original 1940s door to match.

The Husband shuts off the car and stares at the house for a bit.

The Wife lies back in her seat. She's looking up at the ceiling.

"So, what was the plan?" asks The Husband. "Were you two going to just run away together? Did you leave that conference thinking that you'd each divorce your spouses and then work side by side with each other, get married, and nothing bad would happen?"

She shakes her head. A tear rolls down the side of her face. "I don't know."

"Tell me. What'd he say to convince you?"

She huffs in disbelief. "He said he was in an unhappy marriage, that they worked on it for years and nothing ever changed. That his wife was cold hearted and self-absorbed." She fiercely wipes the side of her eye. "I don't know…it just made me happy."

The Husband sighs. "You graduated in three years, social worker with a 4.0 average, then a year to get your master's in the same field with a 4.0. How did you fall for the oldest, most cliché line in the book?"

"I know…it's stupid."

"Yeah…I'll agree with you on that one." He jumps out of the car and goes inside the house. He paces from the family room, through the narrow hall, into the dining room with the high-top table, and then back into the living room.

The Wife is sitting on the edge of the couch. Her shoulders are slumped forward and tears drip from her face. She shakes her head. "I've hurt so many people."

Something softens in The Husband. His wife, with her short hair pulled back, and heart-shaped face, is in honest pain.

She continues, "Last night, my mom and dad asked if I was suicidal." She purses her lips a moment and shrugs. "I confidently told them no. But now, I just want to die. I want to kill myself."

The Husband kneels and looks up at her.

She tries to turn her head away.

He gently holds onto her thighs. Calmly, he says, "Bubby, yeah… there're a lot of people in pain right now. This all can be fixed. We can heal from this. Killing yourself will only spare you the pain.

The rest of us'll have to suffer what's happened as well as the loss of you."

She falls back onto the couch and uses her arm to cover her eyes as she weeps.

"Bubby…" He climbs over the armrest and works his way up the couch to place his forehead on hers. "I love you. God loves you. We can make it through this. I forgive you."

"How?" She pulls her arm away and he lifts his head. Even in her sadness, he can't help but see how beautiful she is. Memories of their time together, vacations, all the years, solidify his feelings for The Wife, his wife.

"Because I love you."

Her sad yet pretty brown eyes lock onto his face. "How are you so calm?"

"Bubby." He puts his head back on her forehead. "Don't you see? We're the yin and yang. When you have bad seasons, I'm there for you. When I have bad seasons, you're there for me."

It takes her a moment to register it all, and then she kisses him. He closes his eyes and it's as powerful as their first kiss. It's real, authentic, true love. She wraps her arms around his shoulders and he lifts them both to their feet.

When they stop for a moment to breathe, he sees in her an instant of authenticity. It feels like it has been forever since he saw that in her face. It's that sunrise smile.

April 12, 2017 – Wednesday

The Husband cooks dinner in the kitchen they gutted and rebuilt. Dark oak stock cabinets that he, The Dad, and his cousin stained and varnished hang on the walls. Olive-colored countertop covers them. It's a tight kitchen with barely enough room for the two of them.

"Hey." The Wife steps into the arched doorway into the dining room.

The Husband asks, "How was your day?"

She's wearing a tight pair of light grey slacks and a maroon top. Her hair is short, colored a light brown, a crop cut, parted on the side, and tucked behind her ears. There's a moment of hesitation before she takes a deep breath and rubs her palms on her thighs. "It was good. I had a good conversation with my boss."

"Oh? What about?" He pulls away from the fry pan and leans one hand on the edge of the counter.

"Well." She turns her attention downward to pick at the skin of her fingertips. "He doesn't want me, or my coworker fired. He met with a board member today who said that either we both stay or we both go."

The Husband sharply twists his chin upward to the left as he returns to the skillet. "So, what's that mean?"

"Well, The Boss is going to fight so he doesn't lose either of us."

A tidal wave of anger and frustration washes over him. He tries to stand firm against the oncoming tsunami. "He thinks you'll both be working together?"

"That's how…it…looks…"

The Husband clicks off the oven top. He takes a deep breath then steps back toward the sink on the opposite side of The Wife. He clenches his teeth. Lightly, he brushes his knuckle on the right side of his jaw a few times.

She looks up and concern fills her eyes. "What are you thinking?"

"I um…" He closes his eyes and shakes his head. "What am I supposed to do?"

"What do you mean?" She crosses her arms, steps out from underneath the arch and leans against the wall.

"I mean…" The flood comes faster. It's getting hard to breathe, as if he has forgotten how to. Every lungful catches somewhere in his chest and won't release. "What would you do if you were me?"

"I don't know." She shrugs and turns her gaze to the oven top on her left.

"I mean," he rubs the back of his neck and digs his fingernails in for just a moment. "You had an affair with him and now you're going to work with him."

Frustration taints her reply. "I know." Then she returns to a more neutral tone, which borders on encouragement. "You're strong. I don't know how you're able to handle all of this."

He gasps in a half chuckle. "I don't either." All sorts of thoughts rush through his head, but mostly he thinks what a horrible husband he must be. "I um…I don't like it…it doesn't make me comfortable."

"I know." She tries to make eye contact with him. "But I don't see him the same way now. He stays far away and acts like we're total strangers. I've lost all respect for him."

The first question that runs through The Husband's mind is, *How am I supposed to trust that?* But he doesn't ask. He grips the edge of the counter behind him. He's deathly afraid to ask the only question he really wants to ask. His eyes begin to burn, and he fights back more crying.

"What are you thinking?"

"I…um." He turns his attention to the ugly vinyl tile on the floor. They didn't have enough money to replace it. He hates it, but at least the tiles match the room. "I um…" He meets her stare. "If I were to step away…" He can't believe what he's asking. "If I were to just leave you with everything, the house, and you could just have a clean-cut separation? Would you take that option?"

She hesitates. "That's a complicated question." The Wife pushes away from the wall. "I don't know. Maybe."

Blackness fills The Husband's vision. He feels himself falling to the floor. Uncontrollable wails erupt, preventing him from inhaling.

The Wife is at his side. "I'm sorry. I just can't say yes or no right now. If it makes you feel any better, it's closer to yes than no."

He shakes his head. Under his breath he says, "God, please kill me.

Kill me right now. I can't handle this. Not this again, God. Please don't put me through this."

After dinner he lies on the couch for the remainder of the night. His body is drained. He refuses to climb out of it.

The Wife stands over top of him. She asks, "Are you going to come to bed?"

He looks away from her. More tears drip down his face. "I can't share a bed with someone who doesn't want to be my wife."

She doesn't say a word and disappears into the other room. The Husband stays on the couch. He finds a corner of the room to stare at. The streetlight casts an eerie yellow into the room through the slit in the curtains covering the bay window.

He pulls the enormous scrapbook of his life from the shelf in his head. All night he kicks himself for pushing The Wife away, for everything, for being a horrible husband. He hates The Boy inside of him, the scrapbook of endless faces of disapproving teachers, classmates, exes, and in-laws. He reads every cutout quote—lines and lines about how he is a loser.

The morning sun slowly rises and beams through the slit in the curtains. There's movement in the hall. The Wife hovers over him. With sincere sadness, she asks, "Can I climb in with you for a little bit?"

He wants to say no, but seeing her moves him deeply. He loves her too much to say no. All he has wanted for days, weeks, is the sincere love she had showed him for so many years. He scoots to the side.

She's tiny enough to fit on the edge of the couch with him. Not a word is exchanged between them. He just wraps his arm around her and holds her tight. This has all happened to him before. He knows where it leads and that he is going to lose the most valuable person to ever enter his life.

April 13, 2017 – Thursday

In the morning, The Wife acts as if she did nothing to crush his spirit the night before. He makes them breakfast. She comes into the kitchen and he gives her a hug. While he serves some eggs and sweet potatoes, he asks, "Could you tell your boss your side of the story today... please?"

Her brow furrows. "I don't know how that'll help anything."

They both sit at the table. "Please...I just feel you need to tell your side of the story. Right now, he only has your coworker's side. What's he said?"

"Nothing bad." She picks at an egg. "Is it that important to you?"

"Yes."

"OK... If it's important to you. I'll try and talk to him about it." She shovels some of the eggs into her mouth. "I have a busy day."

"Thank you."

They eat their breakfast and say goodbye. The Husband spends the day searching for jobs and a surgeon. He doesn't know how much of an issue the toxic thyroid is causing him.

All day, he prays to God, "Please let her make the right decision. Please help her do the right thing. Just this one thing to prove she's in this marriage and that she's not just stringing me along."

At four, she calls. She's on her way to a meeting. "Hey, I'm just calling to check in. How are you?"

"I'm OK." His heart is racing so he steps outside onto the concrete front porch. The fresh air helps. "How was your day?"

"Good. I worked on scholarships all day with The Boss. Now I'm off to a meeting then I'm heading to a friend's."

His ears are ringing. "Did you talk to him about you and the conference and your relationship?"

"No...I was too busy."

There is a long period of silence. The Husband's knees buckle, and he sits.

She says, "OK...well I'm here. I'll call you when I'm done."

"Hey..."

"Yeah?"

"Can you cancel plans with your friend and come home?"

"Is everything OK?"

No, he is deeply pained. "Yeah...I just need to talk."

"OK?" She doesn't say anything for a second. "I'll text her. I probably won't be home until later either way."

"That's fine." But it wasn't.

"Bye...love you..."

It hurts him to say, "I love you too."

They hang up. He packs clothing, some things he uses on a regular basis, toiletries, and the essentials into his car. He spends the rest of the night rehearsing a speech.

The Wife comes home. Her eyes are wide, frightened. "Are you OK?"

Without a word, he takes her by the hand and leads her into the bedroom and has her sit on the edge of the bed. He kneels in front of her and looks up at her as he did on Monday.

He starts his rehearsed, but fragmented speech. "I needed you to do the right thing today, no matter the cost of the job, for us. You were too busy. That seems like your excuse for everything. I needed you to advocate for me and you don't even know if you want me in this home."

She is weeping. "Does this mean it's over?"

"I guess." He rubs the back of his neck. "Unless you can choose me completely. But do it quickly. I'm not going to be tortured like last time. Search God and make the right decision."

He walks out of the room. A part of him wants her to stop him, to tell him, "Don't. Wait. I choose you. We'll work this out together." But she does not. He goes through the front door, slides into his car, and backs away from his true love.

He drives out to The Family Friend's house. She's a short and high spirited older woman who has suffered her fair share of tragedies. He tells her everything that has happened. She shares her life's story with him, down to her cheating husband. The Family Friend encourages him to trust in God. That's all he can do at this point.

That night he lies in an unfamiliar bed, in an unfamiliar house, alone. This is what it is going to feel like. There is no way to avoid it. He prays to God that it isn't true. That it will work out and they will be married happily ever after. His eyes close tiredly as he repeats the same thing.

He will spend two nights in that room before he moves back into his childhood bedroom.

April 17, 2017 – Monday

Easter Sunday convinces The Husband that they need to work on things and that God would be there to heal them and see them through this difficult time.

The Husband text messages The Wife throughout the day. She tells him that she met with the marriage counselor they had before they got married, from the church where they first met. Her Easter was good, and she is feeling a lot more confident in God's will for her life.

That evening, he tries to fall asleep in a hard queen-size bed in his parents' basement. He's in his childhood room. They've changed the paint to light brown and bear decorations cover the walls. His old Lego sets are still put together and laid out as decorations. The last time he had to stay here was after the divorce with The Ex. It doesn't bring him comfort.

He continues to pray to God that their marriage will make it through this dark season. Tiredness takes over and he falls asleep. He has nightmares as vivid as reality that The Wife is in danger.

Panic wakes him, and it feels as if bugs are running wildly across his skin. Without a thought, he puts on his clothing, climbs into his car, and drives home. He prays for his wife the entire time.

The house is dark. Only the streetlamp illuminates it. He quietly lets himself in and walks to the bedroom.

The Wife wakes trembling.

He tells her, "It's OK. I'm sorry. I just had this nightmare where you were in danger and I couldn't shake it."

"It's OK." She looks up at the ceiling. "You just scared me."

"I'm sorry." He breaks down and asks, "Can I stay a little bit?"

She says, "Sure," and then flips the sheets back from his side.

He climbs into bed and rests his head on her chest. He can smell the perfume from their honeymoon.

She rubs the back of his head because that comforts him. "Do you remember the dream?"

"Someone broke in with a knife. I tried to help, tried to call out to you but couldn't."

"It's OK…" She continues to rub his head. "I'm safe."

He tries to get his mind off of it. Nothing he does helps.

She asks, "How was your day back at the school?"

"Tiring. The kids were still on a spring break high. I spent the entire day trying to keep them from hanging from the ceiling. How about you?" He turns his head up to see her.

With her eyes closed, she says, "Good. Just more scholarship stuff and I met with the church counselor."

"How'd that go?"

"It was good." She opens her eyes for a moment and stares at the ceiling. "Yesterday's service was really good. I could feel the Holy Spirit moving, you know?"

"Same here."

"Good…" She tries to look down at him. "I spent the entire weekend worried about you. I don't want you to go through any more pain. God reassured me that you'll be OK. That He has you and I need to work on myself."

"That's good, right?"

"Yeah…I met with the church counselor and it was a really good conversation."

He snuggles up to her. A still small voice tells him that it wasn't a good conversation, that there are forces united against him. He tries to ignore it. "What'd you talk about?"

"Oh…that it's OK to get a divorce and that we need to for each other's mental health."

"What?" He sits upright. "Are you serious?"

Her eyes are wide. "Yeah. God told me to get a divorce."

Red blurs his vision and his ears are ringing. He grips the sides of his head and plants his bare feet on the cold wooden floor. "No…this can't be."

In an instant she goes from comforter to cold and careless. "You said it Thursday. I shouldn't string you along. I'm not going to."

He paces in the small space between the door and the bed. "No… no…no…God wouldn't tell you that."

"He did."

The Husband fishes his phone out of his pocket and calls his dad. It is noon in the Philippines. He puts it on speaker.

The Dad answers, "Hello?"

"She says God told her to get a divorce."

"What? Where are you?" The Dad acts befuddled.

The Husband explains. While he does, that Gollum personality comes out of The Wife. She is hissing, "Put down the phone. Hang up."

The Dad gets the idea. "Should you really be having this conversation so late at night?"

Still pacing, The Husband says, "Yes! She's telling me that the church counselor said it's OK to get a divorce."

The Dad addresses The Wife. "What exactly did the church counselor say?"

The Wife growls, "Hang up the phone." She claws for it, but The Husband pulls away. She gives up, falls back against the headboard, then yells, "I don't want to be ganged up on!"

"No one is ganging up on you," says The Dad. "I'm not taking any sides. I just want some clarification."

The Wife angrily yells, "She said that under the case of abuse God makes allowances for divorce."

"Well that's ignorant. The Bible doesn't say that." He turns his attention to The Husband. "Now, why're you there tonight having this conversation. You don't need to be."

"I had a nightmare that she was in trouble and came over."

"Well...isn't it a good sign that she let you in the house?"

She slams her hands on the bed. "I didn't let him in! He just forced his way!"

Shock smacks The Husband back a step. Just a few minutes ago she was stroking the back of his head, and now she is gnashing her teeth, calling him an abuser and acting like he broke into his own house.

"Now, son, can you agree that tomorrow is a better time to have this conversation, and that no one is going to get a divorce tonight?"

"Yes." The Husband is completely mystified.

The Dad asks The Wife, "Can you agree that no decisions have to be made tonight, that it can be discussed tomorrow?"

"Yes please! I need to work in the morning." She crosses her arms and fumes.

The Dad says, "OK then. Why don't you both get some sleep? Is it OK if your husband stays the night? I would feel more comfortable if he isn't driving at one in the morning."

"I guess." She throws the covers over her shoulder and turns her back to him.

"OK," says The Dad, "I love you both. God will get you through this. Trust Him. Now get some sleep. Goodnight."

The Husband says, "Goodnight."

The Wife huffs.

He cautiously returns to the bed. Her outburst adds another caption to his mental scrapbook: "Abuser." He tries to forget about it and desperately wants to wrap her in his arms. It's what he loves doing the most, but tonight he can't.

April 18, 2017 – Tuesday

The Husband stands with phone to ear underneath a tall tree. Behind him is the charcoal house with the plum shutters. He paces underneath the old oak. The Husband explains the situation to The Pastor.

He asks, "Can you come and be a third party? Tell her what scripture says?"

The Pastor asks, "When?"

"Tonight?"

"Yes, but I need you to understand something." He takes a moment as papers rustle in the background. "If you are honestly doing your best to make this work, if you are truly trying to give her a voice, then I'm going to come down hard on you."

"I understand. I don't want her to ever feel ganged up on."

"Good…see you tonight."

He hangs up the phone and texts The Wife the details as he wanders into the house and then to the kitchen. He prepares steaks, fries, and a salad. He walks around the high-top dining table, out the back door, and down the steps to the patio. It's made of grey block concrete that he put in a few years ago. The grass of the yard around it is already looking long and will need to be mowed soon.

He passes the six-person patio table with chairs, which was a hand-me-down from The Coworker. It doesn't bother him, not today. He prepares the dinner and sets the table before The Wife comes home.

She steps through the back door and closes it behind her. It matches the rich purple they used to paint the shutters and front door. She tucks her phone in a back pocket and then crosses her arms.

He acts overjoyed to see her. "Hey, Bubby! How was your day?"

"Good." She looks out toward the setting sun. "When is he supposed to get here?"

"Anytime really." The Husband pulls out a seat for her. She sits opposite of him.

He forces himself to eat.

She doesn't make the same effort. "How do you know him?"

"I don't." He cuts some of his steak into cubes. "I went to his church Sunday and met him there."

Near the end of the meal, the doorbell rings. He jumps up and says, "I'll get it." The Husband climbs the steps, walks through the dining room and into the living room.

The Pastor stands behind the screen door with Bible in hand. He's young-looking with thick peppered black hair. There's something about his smile that's sincere. It strikes The Husband just how charitable this pastor is. He hardly knows The Husband or The Wife but is willing to make a house call.

The Husband eagerly greets him and opens the screen door. "Come on in, we're around the back."

"Thank you." The Pastor does his best to fit by the broad husband in the narrow walkway created by the ornate dresser and back of the couch. He comments on the house.

"It was a lot of work. A labor of love." The Husband shows him to the back door. They step outside and The Wife stands to shake The Pastor's hand.

They exchange pleasantries. He tells his life story and they regale him with the story of how they met. The Husband brags on The Wife. She is cold and distant. Then The Pastor reads a passage in Mark. He pulls verse after verse as evidence that divorce is never acceptable.

The Wife's eyebrows contort.

Then The Pastor says, "The interesting thing about marriages back then is that there would be a certification of marriage first. Then the bride and groom were technically married, but not joined together as one in his household. They both had to prepare, and that could take years. That's why the Bible talks about the bride-groom. Anyway, the point is that the only way Moses permitted a certification of divorce was during that waiting period when the two people were preparing for the wedding day."

The Wife is silent.

The Pastor turns to her. "Now we could talk to you about scripture all night. Your husband called me because he's willing to do anything to make things right by you and God."

She sits back in her chair. A scowl is frozen on her face. She begins with the same litany she gave him the Saturday she came back from the conference. Then she starts to cry. "Your cynicism is tiring. And your depression is out of control. I spent most of this winter not wanting to come home from fear of not knowing if you were happy or depressed. It was better to stay at work."

The Husband hangs his head. "I'm sorry."

"Your anxieties are out of control. You're so afraid to do anything. I made a spreadsheet so you could record your contacts for your book and you used it once. You're not driven. You complain about your job, but you don't apply yourself hard enough to find another one. Then you make me feel guilty as if I'm forcing you to work crappy jobs." She grips the edge of the glass table, spreading her fingers on top.

The Husband replies, "I'm sorry."

"You try and rationalize my emotions." She lets go with one hand and reaches up to touch her forehead. "If the reason why I'm crying doesn't make sense, if...if I can't explain my feelings in detail to you, then they aren't legitimate."

Whether he agrees with her or not, he says, "Please forgive me."

"I spent nights in your arms crying because I was so depressed." Her fingers are starting to turn white. "You're always comparing me to your ex. I feel like...like I'm never good enough for you...that I can't make you happy. And you're..."

They are all quiet for a moment. The Pastor nudges her to continue.

She nearly yells, "And you're so narcissistic! I honestly believe you have a narcissistic personality disorder."

The scrapbook from The Husband's mental bookshelf opens and a new picture is taped down. It's one of an angry wife with the caption underneath, "You have a narcissistic personality disorder."

The Pastor holds up his index finger and demands, "What is your response?"

"I'm sorry…I didn't know…please forgive me…"

She's done. Everything she's wanted to say just came spilling out and there was someone there to witness it.

April 19, 2017 – Wednesday

The Husband's mind is spiraling out of control. He experiences moments of physical weakness. Early in the morning, near the end of second period, he leans over the desk to grade papers but the fog consumes his vision. He sweats and feels faint, so he sits back and turns his head into the air. His body goes limp.

The third period bell rings. His eyes slowly blink. The light from the window behind him burns. The spots of the sponge ceiling tiles take forever to focus. He slowly sits upright. A few of the middle school students giggle, but it doesn't slow their exit to the next class.

After work he meets The Wife at the house. There is a distance in her eyes, as if she's looking past him. He greets her. She kindly returns his greeting then asks, "Do you want to go for a walk with me?"

"Yeah." It takes him a lot of effort to smile. He follows her into the bedroom and sits on the bed while she changes. She has a strong body. Five years of lifting weights has packed on some attractive muscle. He tries not to stare at her. "How was work?"

She walks into her closet and starts putting away clothing. "Good. I presented some work I've been doing to the board. They were impressed. My boss is confident that when they learn what happened, they'll let it go."

"That's good, right?"

"Yeah." She slips on some shorts and an athletic tank top. Then she rests one hand on her hip and asks, "So what did you want to talk about?"

He stands, places his hands on her shoulders. His heart races out of control. Red fills his vision and he begins to cry openly. His knees buckle, and he falls to the hard wood floors. His palms rest upward on his thighs. He begs for forgiveness, that he's so sorry for everything. He repeats himself a lot and it's muffled by his shaking sobs.

When he regains his composure, she says, "Come on, let's go for a walk."

They start their normal trek down the street with ranch homes on one side and corn fields on the other. Then they walk onto MVNU campus and start a loop around the campus. The breath has returned to The Husband.

He asks, "What did you think of The Pastor?"

"He was nice enough, but I disagree with him."

The Husband refutes this and then the argument escalates. They argue about it past the oversized chapel building, the square three-story brick science building, around the tennis courts, by the volleyball field, and in front of the new sports center. The more they argue the more heated she becomes.

She is angrier than him. In fact, he is in shock, complete disbelief.

Finally, she yells, "I know God told me to get a divorce. If I'm wrong, He can strike me dead!"

April 20, 2017 – Thursday

In the morning, after another night without sleep, he stops at the house. She isn't ready for work yet. School starts far earlier than her work day. He asks, "Did you spend some time praying about us last night?"

She asks, "Why are we playing this game?"

"It's not a game. This is our marriage. Our covenant."

She rolls her eyes.

The Husband bites his lip and angrily prays, "Lord, please be with us today. Please help us control our anger and not do or say anything to hurt the other. Don't let us sin in our hurt. And Lord, like she said last night, if You told her to get a divorce, then send hell's hounds to our door and prove it."

She completely freezes.

He kisses her on the cheek. "I'll be back later in the evening."

The Wife says nothing as he leaves her in the cold living room.

After school, The Husband moves back into their house.

◆◆◆

Around sunset he hears her roll into the driveway. She's not alone in her vehicle and two other cars pull up to the house. He scrambles to put on his clothing. They all begin to climb out of their cars. It's the Mother-In-Law, two mutual friends, and The Wife.

The Husband steps outside, lifts his hands to surrender, and says, "I don't want to fight anymore. Let's just go back to our lives. We can work on counseling and—"

Furious, she interrupts him. "Why are you here?" She stands at the bottom of the steps. Her face is flushed red.

"What? I live here."

"No." She smacks her left palm with the back of her right hand. "You moved out."

"I moved back."

She shakes her head. "You're not allowed to be here."

The Husband is stunned. The two friends with the Mother-In-Law fan behind her. He asks, "Who told you that?"

"My lawyer."

"What?" He has been through a separation before and knows she's wrong. "That's not true."

She marches past him. "Then I'm moving out. This is over. I want a divorce."

He follows her. The Mother-In-Law and two friends, The Henchmen, are in tow.

The Husband begs, "Please don't do this. This isn't right."

She stomps into the bedroom and tosses a basket on the bed. As she feverishly fills it, she says, "It's over. Face it. Our marriage has never been good. I can never make you happy, and lately you've not made me happy."

The Henchmen saunter into the room.

The Husband is destroyed, there's nothing he can do. "How can you say that? These have been the best years of my life. We've had some really good times."

She stops packing and emphatically says, "Some but not enough." Then she continues her process.

The Husband is panicking. Pressure builds behind his ears. He can't get them to pop. "Listen, we can work this out. God will help us—"

"No. We are both too sick for each other. We aren't good together. I need to take care of my mental health and we'll never be healthy."

"That's not true."

She shakes her head and stops arguing.

The Husband's knees buckle and knock him to the floor. He is shaking. He begs The Henchmen, "Please don't let her do this. You know it's wrong. You know this is wrong."

The Male Henchman says, "Honestly, you're acting incredibly manic right now, and the things I've heard you do over the past couple of weeks are entirely out of line."

"What?" The Husband grips his temples and shakes his head. "She had an affair! I have no support system in town."

They both glare disapprovingly.

Somewhere amid the packing, The Husband goes outside to the minivan parked on the front lawn where The Father-In-Law sits and waits. The Husband begs and pleads with The Father-In-Law. The man is weak; he just tears up, and won't take any side.

The Husband goes back inside, sits in a chair, puts his hand to his forehead and does his best not to cry. The worst moment of his life is playing out in front of an audience who, aside from The Father-In-Law, spectates in disdain.

A Long Time before April 20, 2017

Every time The Boy tried to ask a teacher for help, he'd end up in trouble. It didn't matter if he fought or tattled on the bullies, he was sent to The Principal's office. There he sat across from the disapproving glare of his grouchy principal. A giant wood desk separated them. The room was dark with an American Flag in the corner.

The Principal was bald with brown age spots. He was always sharply dressed in a blazer and tie. He'd look down so he could see The Boy over the rim of his circular framed glasses.

The Gym Teacher, a bulky stupid-looking man, would stand in front of the flag with his arms crossed. This was the man who marched the kids back to class, and harassed the student he disliked the most. Often, it was The Boy. The Gym Teacher body shamed The Boy the most in these moments, and his insults sparked the bullies' creativity.

The only difference from one principal's office visit to another was who flanked his other side. It was usually a teacher who played the prosecutor. Often, it was The Snow-Haired Teacher who spit her hatred. She would stop at The Boy's house on her way home to tell his parents how horrible their child was.

Sometimes it was the second-grade teacher who put all of the students' academic and behavioral digressions on the board for the entire class to see. She used public humiliation to correct The Boy's behavior. She often made him feel stupid and rarely acknowledged his complaints about being bullied. Her response was something akin to, "How can the biggest kid in the classroom be bullied?"

Even the Art Teacher contributed to this negative atmosphere. He was a short man with black combover hair and a funny walk. When The Boy asked for late work after one of his annual suspensions, the Art Teacher bent down to look The Boy in the eyes and said, "Horrible little children who get suspended don't get to make up work they missed. You're a thug. I wouldn't worry about the assignment. You'll be in prison before you graduate high school."

Back to April 20, 2017 – Thursday

At the end of The Wife's packing, she returns to the family room tailed by her Henchmen. Cold and indifferent, she looks around, and without empathy asks, "Is that it?"

The Husband lifts his heavy body from the chair and asks, "Can we say a prayer?"

The Wife huffs and rolls her eyes.

The Father-In-Law suddenly gains sentient life and says, "It's always a good time to pray." He holds out his hands and everyone forms a circle. He opens with prayer. What he says doesn't register. The Husband prays incoherently for forgiveness, healing, and that God will bring them both together.

Everyone appears solemn as the prayer ends and hugs are distributed to The Husband. To each person he wraps his arms around he says, "Please take divorce off the table." When he hugs The Wife, he repeats himself and says, "I love you."

Like a trapped cat, she squirms away from his hug and says, "I love you too."

The Husband repeats himself to The Henchmen and they pretend to be concerned.

They all exit the house. From the crack in the curtain, The Husband watches as their demeanor changes from solemn to gleeful, nearly high fiving each other. They giggle as they climb into the car.

The minute they drive off, The Husband calls his parents. He can't stop pacing. Anger causes him to yell all the details of the evening to his helpless parents.

Then he begins to drink, one after another. He just wants his heart to stop beating. He wants to be able to end his uncontrollable pacing. His parents beg him to quit drinking, but he can't. They call The Family Friend to come to the house. The Husband is six hard ciders and half a bottle of tequila in before he bumps into the wall and crashes to his knees. He is wailing into the phone.

The Family Friend arrives, and The Parents coax him to open the door. He staggers up the wall. He braces himself on the edge and back of the couch as he works his way to the front door and opens it. The Family Friend half smiles.

The Husband returns to the center of the hallway and drops his phone. The room is spinning but his ears have finally popped. He scoots himself against the wall and repeatedly asks God, "Why?"

His parents call out to him but he won't pick up the phone. The Family Friend does and together, they urge him to drink water. The Family Friend calls The Husband's best friend who lives in Oregon. The two talk for hours. The Bestie keeps asking, "Bestie…bestie…will you drink some water for me?" The rest is a blur of total blackness.

April 21, 2017 – Friday

The Family Friend spends the night sleeping in a small chair across from the sofa. He remembers waking up a couple times and telling her to sleep in the bed, but she says she is OK.

His cell phone rings. It's his parents so he answers. The Dad is ecstatic. The Husband is still drunk. The Dad has gotten ahold of a lawyer who is ready to take the case with no upfront cost.

The Family Friend drives him to Columbus for a therapy session. The Husband calls The Lawyer. The Lawyer says, "Go to the bank and pull out half the money from your joint account."

The Husband is the good zombie from his youth and does as he is told. At the bank he learns that The Wife pulled out a large chunk of their savings on Monday after her meeting with The Ignorant Counselor, and another large chunk that morning.

The Zombie takes the rest because the last time he checked with her, there was double what it appeared she had taken out of the account. He walks away with a considerably large check. The Lawyer tells him to text this to his wife. He does. "I took out the money you left behind in both accounts. You'll need to deposit something into the savings if you don't want it to bounce."

He makes it to the counseling session but feels completely defeated.

This is not what he wants. He doesn't care about the money, or anything except being with his wife.

At one point, he holds the check out to The Therapist and says, "You want this? I don't even care about it. I feel like burning it. I can't help but think this entire thing is about money and how I can't make enough."

Then his phone explodes with messages from his wife. "How could you do that to me?? I can't pay anything. I can't pay any of our bills. Nothing at all. I am paying your loans. Your car. The house. Phone. Internet."

His reply: "I did what my lawyer told me to do. I can give you his number and you can ask him."

Her reply: "How am I supposed to pay for anything? Any of our bills?" There is a long break between messages and she writes, "Give me the number."

She tries to call The Husband, but he doesn't want to talk to her. She texts, "Where are you? I just can't even believe you. I can't pay our credit card bills. Our mortgage. Electric. Internet. Anything. You need to take on those bills through your account now. And answer my calls." The Zombie is hit hard, to his core. Everything he has been anxious about over the past year rings true in The Wife's one text.

She blows up his phone. "I'm your parent's POA, what if I took money from them? You left me pennies. I trusted you wouldn't do something like this." A break in messages then, "Trusted."

The Zombie refuses to reply.

The Wife continues, "I took half out, which I was going to claim. And I'm still paying everything out of those accounts. I offered to take you to start a new account for yourself. You took EVERYTHING I/we have ever earned."

She never made such an offer.

There is a pause of about an hour and then she messages, "And by claim I mean, I wasn't trying to hide it. You were told to take half. What you took out is not half. And is this an example of Christ-like behavior? Don't lecture me and then do this. I have taken care of you financially for years. I've paid your parents' bills. And you don't even leave me enough money to pay our bills for the past month. And that will come back on me because everything is in my name. I've taken responsibility for everything over the years. Please just take some responsibility now."

He's worthless to her, a loser. All his work on the house, it's meaningless. To her, he is a burden. He just wants to stay married. He yearns to work things out with The Wife and move forward. By the end of that Friday, all the money is figured out and he returns most of what he removed. She was not thankful or kind about it.

The Zombie begins to make plans to kill himself.

April 22, 2017

The Zombie wakes from another drunken stupor. He's on the couch and drool has solidified on the side of his face. It's five in the morning and the sun hasn't begun to rise. He's alone.

At some point during the day yesterday, while he was in Columbus, The Wife came to the house, took his phone charger, his laptop, the cat, and unplugged the garage door. The latter baffles him as he sits, rocking, alone, in the dark.

In that moment, he prays, "God...I'm done...I'm destroyed...I can't go on with this pain...it's too great. I've struggled so long. I'm so tired." Then suicide dawns on him.

He drinks more tequila to take off the woozy feeling. Then he digs out paper and a pen. He writes to The Parents, to The Bestie, to The Brothers, and lastly to The Wife. The message to The Wife essentially reads, "I'm so sorry for everything I've done to you. It feels like I've failed an exam where I was never taught the content. I didn't know what I was doing at the time. I can't forgive myself for this. You deserve better. I know the only way you can get away from the situation, hands clean, is if I kill myself. Then you'll be able to keep everything without a fight, and be able to point at me and say I was crazy."

He grabs his favorite picture of the two of them, the only one to survive with frame intact, and goes to his closet, fishes out a belt. The Zombie drags himself to the basement, the home gym. It has two full power lifting racks, barbells, a few dumbbells, and a couple of benches.

He scoots a bench to the pull-up rack. Climbing on top is already a challenge. He slides the long leather belt through the buckle but doesn't let it fasten. Using the bench for a boost, he strings the belt to the top bar and hangs on it for a bit. It will hold. The buckle creates a loop that will tighten and tighten until he stops breathing.

Then he climbs down, moves the bench back, lays out his letters, and stands up his favorite picture of the two of them. The Zombie can hardly recognize the people in it. The frame mockingly reads, "Faith and Family."

Like an actual zombie, he crooks his head and tries to remember that time in his near-dead brain. He can recall it vividly. It was one of their first dates. He feels the heat from the sun, watches the tall grass wave, and the people on the top of the hill looking down at the same valley. The wind was out of control. They asked some strangers to take a photo, and in one near impossible moment, they captured a perfect picture of the cheesy grinning man and a sunrise smile of a woman as a couple.

In his last moment, after another swig of tequila, he types in his phone's search engine, "What does the Bible say about suicide?" He finds an article on how suicide doesn't mean you'll go to hell. So he is convinced. In moans and gasps he prays, "God, stop me if you want me to live." Then there is nothing.

He knows this is the right thing to do. After all, he is a monster, a thug, a horrible person, the abuser, narcissistic, so awful that no one can stand him. History keeps repeating the same words spoken from different mouths. He has the scrapbook to prove it. The Wife deserves to be free of him. He deserves to die. In a moan he says, "Everyone will be better off when I'm dead."

The Zombie rocks on his heels and prepares to pull himself into the homemade noose. The phone rings. Curiosity piques. He did just say that prayer.

It's The Parents. His first inclination is to ignore them, but a still small voice tells his dead brain to answer to hear his loving parents' voices one more time. He answers. They tell him The Youngest Brother has taken the day off from work and will be there soon.

The Zombie's attention focuses on the noose. He does not want his brother to walk into the mess of his older brother's suicide. Not knowing exactly when The Brother will be there, he unties the belt, folds up the picture, hides the notes in the notebook, and then takes everything back upstairs.

Paranoia consumes The Zombie. He doesn't know what The Wife has planned. She's already ganged up on him. He watches a grey truck pass by the house several times and even park in the neighbor's yard. He doesn't feel safe in his own home.

Then his Good Friend, who has friends in the police department, calls. They are close, and he has kind of adopted her into his family. She begins the conversation by asking, "Are you OK?"

He runs his hand across his bald head. "No, I'm a mess. I can't even charge my phone."

"OK, I need you to calm down."

He thinks he is calm.

"Yesterday, when she went to the house looking for you, she had a police escort. Some of the guys told me about it. She's claiming you're a physical danger to her safety."

This knocks The Zombie onto the floor. He can hardly believe it. There's no way he would ever harm The Wife or anyone. He hasn't physically retaliated since he was in fifth grade in that pee-stained bathroom.

He remembers years of being paranoid that he'd lose his temper. He never wants to be that person. In fact, he rarely lost his temper with The Wife. It has been hard to control it the past two weeks, but he can't imagine harming her.

He says, "I've got to get out."

"I'd do that," reaffirms The Good Friend. "Just don't lash out on her."

He hoists himself from the wood floors. "No. I'm not going to. I'm getting as far away from her as possible." The Zombie hangs up the phone and starts chugging water. He begins packing anything he may need inside boxes.

The Family Friend comes over to check on him. She agrees with his plan and helps him pack. Shortly thereafter, The Youngest Brother pulls into the driveway.

He climbs out of the car. His thick black hair is a genetic gift The Zombie never had. He's sporting a scraggly beard these days and has gained some weight over the years. There's something about him that matured. He no longer seems like The Youngest Brother.

The Zombie meets him on the front lawn. The first thing the brothers do is hug. Then they go into the house and begin to start packing the cars with boxes of food, baskets of clothing, and whatever he remembers to grab.

As The Zombie digs through the closet in his room, he finds boxes of every note he and The Wife have shared over the years. He has kept nearly all she's given him. The Zombie stands, frozen with the notes in his arms, trying to remember a life he will never have again.

The Youngest Brother steps into the room. "Do you have anything else?"

"There are some boxes in the kitchen."

"Are you OK?"

The Zombie looks down at the notes and says, "I just need a little time." He begins to carry the notes into the next room and lay them out on the queen-sized bed. He returns to his room and finds three scrapbooks that have chronicled their life together. He opens the first; it's their wedding album.

He feels faint. His knees smash into the ground before he has the chance to realize he is blacking out and fainting. When he wakes, he scoots himself against the wall.

Tears and snot drain from his face as he turns page after page of photos, all those moments he forgot about. Cute little cutouts and lovely quotes in cursive writing are difficult to read with his blurry eyes. Life seems messy at the beginning and endings. The middles are where all the magic happens. Out of all The Zombie's sins, not embracing each new day, with its magnificent sunrise, hurts him the most.

One scrapbook haunts The Zombie. On the first page is a picture of The Wife, gorgeous, in yellow, tan, with that sunrise smile he fell in love with. There's a quote from The Mother. It reads, "My son came to me unsure whether or not he should marry again, if he could trust this girl forever. I told him, 'When a girl as amazing and loyal as this girl comes along, you'd be a fool not to.'"

He struggles to his feet and lays the scrapbook onto the bed. He opens the other two, sobs, and places them on his favorite pages. He digs out all the loose pictures he can find.

One by one he lays them out and steps back to look at it. It's beautiful. Everything about it sears through his heart. In that moment, he knows it's over, forever. This journey has come to an end. He has lost the love of his life.

The Youngest Brother peeks into the room. "The cars are packed. You think you've got everything?"

The question takes a moment to register in The Zombie's dying brain. "I…I need to do one more thing…I need to write a note." He grabs the pad of paper that hides his suicide notes and writes one final note to The Wife. It reads something to the effect of, "I trusted you. I will always love you. I forgive you. What has been done can be undone. All things are possible through God. You will always have my arms to return to."

No matter what he does, the snot and tears won't stop flowing. It takes him a while to remember he can walk. He gently tears off the note and shuffles toward the bedroom. On the way there, through the front bay window, he catches the colors of a police cruiser passing the house. It is being followed by The In-Law's minivan. They pull into the grass. Both The In-Laws are inside, and The Wife opens the side door to step out of the van.

A Little over Two Weeks before April 8, 2017

The Husband sat on an artsy recreation of a grey 1950s couch. Across from him was the EMDR (eye movement desensitization and reprocessing) machine. A horizontal line of green lights turned off and on, bouncing in succession from left to right. He had on earphones that matched the left to right movement with beeps, as well as vibrators in each hand. The smell of coffee filled the air.

The Therapist sat catty-corner to him in a similarly stylized chair. She asked him, "What are you feeling?"

"Worthless...powerless..." For some reason, these sessions made it hard for him to articulate.

"OK," she replied, "where do you feel that?"

"On my chest, shoulders, and neck."

In a gentle tone she said, "Concentrate on that feeling, where it comes from." Then she turned on the device.

The green light bounced from the middle to the left, then to the right back to the left. The devices in his hands vibrated and the earphones beeped in his ears to match the pattern. His mind focused on a vivid memory of the disapproving principal with age spots on his bald head and long nose.

The Principal was sitting across from The Boy. The Snow-Haired

Teacher stood on the left side of The Principal. She was flushed red. Her scraggly finger pointed down at The Boy. She was yelling about something which time had turned to gibberish, white noise, but the intensity and the hate were somehow still present in the wordless static of garbled language.

The hulking giant of a gym teacher with a beer gut was standing on the right side of The Principal. He glared down at the second-grader. As if this old man needed a bodyguard against a small child.

Somewhere, in the mass of indistinguishable dialog, echoed the words, "You're a horrible little boy. You'll never be anything but worthless."

The lights stopped along with everything else. The Therapist asked, "What memories did you encounter?"

The Husband realized he had stopped breathing. It took him a moment to recover and then he described it.

"What feelings are associated with it?"

"The same. Powerlessness, worthlessness, shame. I feel ganged up on and I just want to run away but I can't. That I'm all alone."

"OK." She shifted in her chair. "Where do you feel that?"

"The same. On my chest, shoulders, and neck."

"Concentrate on those feelings." She clicked on the machine.

The light, vibrators, and beeps moved back and forth in rhythm. The memory of that principal's office transformed into the living room from his childhood home. He couldn't tell if he was younger or the same age. It was an echo of so many moments on repeat. The room had that same wood paneling, a brown couch he sat in, and a boxy entertainment system made from particle board in one corner.

The emotional Mom with the rational Dad were standing over top of him. They stood in front of the entrance to the dining room, which had a snot-green carpet. A crystal chandelier hung above a crow-claw table with matching chairs. Light beamed in from a side window. The Boy folded his hands and bowed his head in shame.

The Mom was hurt and confused. The Dad was controlled and analytical. He repeated words that he would repeat even in The Boy's teenage years. "Why don't you think first? I know they hurt you, but you need to think about your actions. They have consequences. You need to learn how to control yourself."

The Mom felt far away. The Boy could tell that they loved him. In that moment, he hated himself. He didn't want to hurt them. He didn't mean to do what he did, whatever it was had merged into the same harmonious emotions. All he knew was that he couldn't control himself.

The light, beeps, and vibrations stopped. The Therapist asked, "What memories did you encounter?"

Tears dripped from The Husband's eyes. The words lodged in his throat. He needed to breathe, powerfully inhale for a count of four, hold for six, and slowly release with a count of eight.

"What do you feel?"

"Horrible...powerless...hurt...worthless...the same. I didn't know what to do. I didn't know how I was acting or why. I was afraid of myself."

She leaned forward. "If you were there, as an adult, what would you tell The Boy? How would you encourage and comfort him? What does The Boy need to hear?"

The Husband looked up at The Therapist. He fought back tears. "I honestly don't know." The breathing no longer held his heart at bay. He began to shake and openly wept.

April 22, 2017

The In-Laws pull their car up onto the grass as the police cruiser passes. Both The In-Laws and The Wife begin to climb out of the van. The Zombie shuffles to the front door. His heart is pounding, he can hardly breathe. Every muscle in his body is twitching as millions of bugs burrow underneath his skin and run in all directions.

His voice is hoarse as he says, "Could my wife please stay in the van while I talk to the two of you?"

The Wife rolls her eyes and climbs back into the van.

Both In-Laws bow their heads as they approach.

The Zombie calls The Youngest Brother to join them. All four move to the center of the living room. The Zombie is shaking. He begins by saying, "I'm sorry for the mess. We didn't have time to clean up, but we planned on it. The rest of the money should be in the joint account. I didn't want to do this, I still love my wife, but I have to protect myself."

The Mother-In-Law huffs and duplicates her daughter's eye rolling.

The huff almost feels physically powerful, like a shockwave into The Zombie's knees. He continues, "What's been done can be undone. God can heal this and us from this."

The Father-In-Law agrees. The Mother-In-Law grumbles and turns her gaze.

"I'm moving out, so she can feel comfortable in the house."

"You are moving out," confirms The Father-In-Law.

"I am." An upsurge knocks into The Zombie. He begins to sob, wail, and he steps into the dining room so he can allow his knees to give way. They smash into the ground. He curls into a ball there and blackness fills his vision. A still small voice tells him to get it together, to get up and get out of the house.

He finds the strength to do so and returns to the hall. In that moment, The Mother-In-Law is the spitting image of The Snow-Haired Teacher. It takes him back to that feeling as The Boy. He continues, "I've talked to my lawyer. Your daughter has been unable to provide him with her lawyer's name, nor has a lawyer contacted him."

They are quiet.

He says, "I'm warning you, he's said that splitting finances without a lawyer involved, getting police escorts without enough cause, doesn't make The Wife look good."

The Mother-In-Law makes a noise somewhere between a disapproving *tsk* and a bestial growl. The Father-In-Law nods his head.

The Zombie finishes by saying, "Let's say a prayer."

The Father-In-Law begins to pray, "We love You, Lord. Please give us Your wisdom and may we know Your will and do what is right." He sounds sincere.

The Zombie prays, "Lord, I know You can heal us all at any stage of this. Forgive us of our sins. Through You, we know what has been done can be undone. Please…"

The Mother-In-Law makes her guttural angry noise.

It bashes The Zombie. It's as if his heart explodes. He quickly retreats into the dining room, uncontrollably wails, and faints. The bugs dig deeper into his skin and worm around like maggots. His entire body convulses.

He finally climbs to his feet and returns to the hall.

The Youngest Brother says, "I asked them to give us a few minutes and they said they would drive around a bit."

The Zombie does his best to compose himself. They gather what else he may need, and drive to his parents' house. It takes them minutes to unpack his life. Boxes are strewn across the basement. The Zombie stands over them.

He tries to remember his achievements. He tries to remember a time he felt, or was, successful. All he can see are boxes filled with junk.

Fall 2016

Those tits of his youth were always there. He ate clean, ran, lifted often, and did nearly everything he could do to get the weight off, but those tits still hung there. He was defeated. For all his knowledge and ability, he could not lose enough weight to make them disappear.

He was stressed. He lost his job as a trainer. Anxiety and depression became anthropomorphic beings and moved into his brain for a permanent stay. Every time he looked in the mirror, he was reminded of how much he proved the bullies right. How he, even as a personal trainer, could do nothing about those stupid tits.

Finally, he found a system that worked. It transformed his body into what he wanted. This did not make him feel any better. He obsessed about his baldness, his acne, stretch marks, his age, whatever he could about his appearance because he became his own bully.

Every achievement he made in life was to prove some frozen picture with a caption wrong. He had to prove to The Art Teacher, The Principal, The Snow-Haired Teacher, and The Gym Teacher, that they were all wrong. He was going to be successful. One day he would get a book published as a "screw you all" for being wrong about him.

Even as he went about his second marriage, he told the image of The Ex, "See you're wrong about me. I'm a good husband." Every house repair, every patio block dropped, every shingle put on the roof was to prove all the bullies wrong.

But he hadn't done enough. He didn't finish a graduate degree. He didn't earn enough money. He wasn't strong enough, lean enough, attractive enough, four novels weren't good enough, an English degree wasn't useful enough. As a husband he was not enough, happy enough, encouraging enough, successful enough, bringing home enough money, selfless enough, thoughtful enough, assertive enough, attentive enough, funny enough, in high spirits enough, or good enough. Enough... enough...enough...

April 23, 2017 – Sunday

The Zombie wakes, cleans himself, puts on his Sunday best.
After church, he returns to hover over his boxes. They are laid out on the floor of his parents' basement. The homemade bookshelves filled with his dad's books are behind them. Between the old books, the things inside the boxes, the dampness of the painted cinderblock walls, there's a smell of mildew. It gags him.

He digs out a Bible, but doesn't open it. None of it really matters to him. Not the house, not the stuff, not the money, none of it is enough. The thought of "enough" is oppressive.

For a moment he wonders if he made his wife feel the same way. He imagines she did. Remembering back, she would say, "I just don't feel like I'm enough for you." Of course, she is. In that moment, she's all he wants.

The Youngest Brother sits up from the couch on the opposite end of the great room. Blankets roll off him and he reaches for his phone on the beechwood coffee table. "Did you go to church?"

Not breaking gaze with the junk, The Zombie replies, "Yeah...want to go get food?"

"Sure, let me get dressed." The Youngest Brother plugs away on his phone.

The Zombie whispers, "God, If I'm an abusive spouse, a narcissist, and too sick to be married to her, please kill me. If you're a God who tells people to get divorces, how can I trust You?" Every second that passes adds another layer of self-hate. "I swear...if You don't...I'll do it myself."

Ruminations of the past two weeks explode in The Zombie's head. As they drive to lunch, a panic attack hits The Zombie. They pull into the parking lot of a grocery store. He shakes and wails. He slams his head against the steering wheel and says, over and over, "I can't do this. I can't do this anymore. I can't handle this pain. I just want to die. I can't go through this again. Call someone or I'll kill myself tonight."

The Youngest Brother calls The Good Friend. She recommends a psychiatric hospital. The Good Friend gives them all the instructions. They return home to pack a bag.

The Family Friend meets them at the house so she can travel with The Youngest Brother to help check The Zombie into the hospital. She's sincere and motherly. They drive over an hour to get there, and check The Zombie into the hospital.

The waiting room has a high roof with floor-to-ceiling front windows. The chairs feel sterile. Lockers line the left side of a heavy double door and the check-in counter is on the right. The Youngest Brother does most of the talking and hands the paperwork to The Zombie.

Not long after, there's a beep and click from the double doors. A short lady with thick glasses steps into the waiting room. She calls The

Zombie's name. It takes him all his energy to get out of that chair. The Youngest Brother and Family Friend stay in the lobby.

Through the double doors, The Lady leads him into a room with three chairs. Two of them are separated by an end table and an industrial-looking lamp. The only other decor is a TV mounted on the wall, locked inside a Plexiglas box.

She begins by taking his blood pressure and temperature. Then she sits next to him with a clipboard. Her voice is calm and pleasant as she goes through a list akin to a twisted online personality quiz.

He tells her the entire story and relives every moment. When they're done, she hums. Then she asks, "Would you like me to bring your family in to see you while I discuss your case with The Doctor?"

He nods yes.

The little lady leaves the room. There is a buzz and click that echoes down the hall. The Zombie puts his head between his legs. Those blurry spots are back. The smell of pee and bleach fills his nose. The yellow standard-issue vinyl tiles with brown marbling belong in a hospital of the deranged.

Both The Family Friend and The Youngest Brother enter the room. She sits on the farthest chair with a deep frown, while he plops into the chair next to the end table. He leans over it and asks, "How're you doing?"

Water builds in The Zombie's eyes. "I'm in a looney bin."

"It's not a looney bin." He talks with a wisdom The Zombie has never imagined could come from The Youngest Brother. "You're finally going to get the help you need. I'm proud of you. This isn't an easy thing to do. It's brave to ask for help."

About that moment, The Zombie realizes his chair rocks forward and back. It adds to the dizziness he feels. The splotches take over his vision. He faints and slides off the chair. When he wakes he is in the corner of the room curled into a ball. The Family Friend is hovering over him.

A nurse, in a blue smock with a long yet gentle and kind face enters. She speaks with an accent. "Are you doing OK?"

Already, he wishes people would stop asking him that. It's hard for him to reply, "The chair was moving too much…I needed solid ground."

The Nurse tilts her head. "Do you need a blanket?"

"No thank you."

The Nurse passes The Youngest Brother and The Family Friend a glance, then she leaves. The Zombie begins to openly cry. It feels like it takes the nurse forever to return.

The little lady says, "OK, honey, we don't have a room ready for you but will tomorrow. The Doctor doesn't want to move you to the hospital and we don't want to put you in a wing you don't belong inside. So, we'll set you up on a nice mattress in solitary. Is that OK?"

He nods yes.

The Lady tells The Youngest Brother they can leave. The Youngest Brother stands, looks down at The Zombie and says, "OK, brother. We're going to go. I'm going to be praying for you."

"Me too," adds The Family Friend.

"Wait." The Zombie uses the last of his strength to pull himself to his feet. "I want to hug you goodbye. He wraps his arms around his brother. A part of him doesn't want to let him go, he doesn't want to be alone.

The Youngest Brother whispers, "I love you, big brother. Be strong."

The Family Friend hugs The Zombie as well and expresses her love. They leave, and the wind is knocked out of The Zombie. He stands there rocking on his heels as The Nurse from earlier comes into the room.

She guides him down the hall and through another key card activated double door, which buzzes and unlocks. They walk into a great room. The yellow tile of the floor is more marbled here. There is an oval of green tile in a line all around the long room. The nurses' station is in the center. The room's ceiling is high with two massive oval sun-lights.

The entire room is dim. In front of and behind the station are seating areas with chairs and a coffee table in the center. The chairs are that hospital vinyl with giant rubber armrests. A few people sit in them. They stop talking and look up at the mess that has just walked through the door. The place seems clean, borderline hotel-like, and appears to be hygienic but feels like a cage.

The Nurse leads him into an adjacent hospital room. There's the long bed with paper on top, a desk, a sink, and charts of medical things on the wall. She draws blood, tests his blood pressure, and heart rate. It's a regular physical. She goes over the paperwork. "It says you have hyperthyroidism?"

He lifts his head to show the lump on his throat.

Her eyes widen, and she begins to feel around it. "You've had it checked?"

"Yeah...they wanted me to have surgery to have it removed."

"And why haven't you?"

He sighs. "My wife told me we didn't have enough money."

"Uh huh." She stops. "Does it hurt?"

"Badly...for the past couple of weeks."

She turns to her table and looks over the paperwork. "Wow." She shakes her head. "And you've been having panic attacks, seizure-like symptoms, fainting?"

"I have an anxiety disorder."

She shakes her head. "You have a toxic thyroid. Those panic attacks are thyroid storms. You should have had at least two heart attacks by now, or worse. Thyroid storms are life threatening." She closes the file and stands. "You're lucky to be alive."

The Zombie's dim brain would hardly call it luck.

PART TWO
THE POINT OF NO RETURN

A Long Time before April 23, 2017

The Boy had seen so many different therapists over the years. There was the fat creepy guy who would turn out all the lights and talk to him in the dark. There was the grouchy woman who would listen to the teacher's gossip and confront him about it. There was the nice one, but he didn't remember spending much time talking to her.

There were two different counselors in college. The first was an extremely tall guy who never remembered The Boy's name. He always referred to The Boy as "Son," and talked about his physical health. The Boy made a game out of repeating the same story to the counselor, tracking how many times it took before the guy caught on, but it ended at seven.

Then there was another grouchy old lady with a crooked eye. She had the blood of a Calvinist and every session ended with a reminder that he was filth in need of repentance. She had altar calls without an altar. The Boy stopped seeing her.

There were four or five others. None of them seemed to add much value to his existence. None of them were able to see the many breaking points of his life. None of the psychiatrists were able to prescribe him the correct cocktail to get his mental imbalances under control.

Out of the many faces, a high school counselor had taught him something. He was an older gentleman, probably close to retirement. It was The Boy's senior year at a career center. The Man had a charming laugh and would engage The Boy in debate as if this youth were some intellectual worth having a discussion with.

The most impactful day, The Man sat back in his squeaky swivel chair. The Man's desk was swallowed by a giant off-white monitor that should have retired long ago. He had aluminum shelves with books and sports things on them. He even had a plaque with a Bible verse on it.

He ran his hand through his thinning hair to make sure the part was in place. He asked, "What happens when they start bullying you?"

The Boy was confused. "What do you mean?"

Using both hands to touch his head he said, "In your mind." This day The Man was wearing a sky-blue shirt and a horizontal tie lined with blues and reds. Then he placed his hand on his chest. "In your heart?"

"I don't really know. My vision kind of gets blurry. I can feel pressure in my ears."

"And what do you want to do? What's your Emotional Mind telling you?"

"I don't know what you mean."

The Man leaned forward on the chair and set his arms on the rests. "I mean what is your first reaction?"

"I um…" The Boy tried to recreate those moments. It was hard. "I want to just run away, out of the room, but I can't. So, I uh…I just sometimes rub the back of my neck. Sometimes I dig my fingernails into my neck. Sometimes my head twitches. I fight back the way I feel."

"Well…that's kind of a good direction." The Man rocked on his toes to square up with The Boy. "I want you to try something different. Close your eyes."

The Boy did.

"Now breathe."

The Boy chuckled, and replied, "I am."

"I mean take a quick powerful lungful for a count of four, hold that breath for a count of six, and then release a long slow breath of seven."

The Boy tried it. The first time it made him a little woozy, but the next few times, calmness filled his muscles.

"OK good," said The Man. "Now I want you to try and clear your mind of all the thoughts. Try and forget about homework…The Bullies…your parents…school…church… Just focus on blankness."

"It's black."

"Good." The Man's chair squealed. "Now I want to focus on a feeling. I want you to focus on the feeling of safety. What that feels like to be at peace. Then I want you to take that feeling and find a place where you can feel it. Then describe it."

Swirled colors and flashed images raced through The Boy's head. He tilted it a little as he tried to remember or create a place in which he felt safe. "I see it."

"Describe it."

"It's a room, not very big. There's a fireplace inside it. It's crackling."

"Good." The Man asked, "Can you smell the wood burning?"

The Boy took a deep breath in the rhythm he was instructed. "Yeah. It's smoky yet sweet. There's the smell of a library mingled in it. It's like a sandstone fireplace. There's a set of black pokers on the side. In front of it is a chair, leather. It's red and kind of Victorian with those buttons all throughout the back."

The Man said, "Very good. Now, where's the library smell coming from?"

"There are books. On the other side is a tall wooden bookshelf with a ladder that slides in front of it."

"What kind of books are on it?"

He tried to read the labels. "Most of them are books I've read. Some are just old-looking. There's an entire row with my name written on it."

"You said you want to be a writer. Are these books you've published?"

The Boy shrugged. "I don't know. I think so. There's a lot of empty space. I need to add more books. At the far end is a window. It's tall. A few trees are in the yard. Their leaves are turning colors, red, yellow, orange. Some of the brown leaves are on the grass. The sky is kind of cloudy. It looks like a comfortable fall day."

"And fall is your favorite season?"

The Boy nodded yes.

"Good. Now I want you to grab a book off the shelf."

"Which one?"

"Any one. Just grab one and have a seat in the chair."

The Boy pictured the bookshelf. There were so many to choose from. He grabbed one with his name on it. It was tall, long, and wide, a huge binder of sorts. Then he sat in the chair in front of the fire.

"Are you in the chair?"

"Yeah." The Boy hodded. "Should I open the book?"

"Not yet. I want you to picture an identical chair right next to you."

The Boy did so without a problem. "Yeah."

"In that chair, I want you to picture Jesus or God sitting next to you."

The Boy strained to picture what Jesus looked like. God came out as just a glowing point of light. Jesus was at least in the shape of a man. He was in a robe and sandals. The Boy tried to make out the face. It looked a lot like Antonio Banderas with long wavy black hair. "OK?"

"Good, hold onto that image." They were silent for a few minutes. Then the man said, "Have a conversation with Him. Talk to Him about The Bullies, the books on your shelf, the one on your lap."

In The Boy's head, Antonio Banderas Jesus laughed at corny jokes. He even made some bad puns. The Boy smiled. Feeling comfortable with the Banderas Jesus, he opened the book to read its contents but was interrupted.

"Open your eyes."

The Boy did. It took his eyes a while to adjust and make out The Man with his thinning hair and blue shirt.

"Now." The Man stood up and pushed his chair underneath the desk.

"Whenever a bully picks on you, when your head gets dizzy and you see red, I want you to escape to that room you created. I want you to picture Jesus sitting next to you. I want you to have a conversation with Him." The Man placed his right hand on The Boy's shoulder. "Give it to Him. Laugh. Read to Him. Read the books you write to honor Him."

That moment solidified in The Boy's mind. Throughout the following years, he would run away to that library whenever he felt overwhelmed. It took him a while to get it right. He even had a few slipups where he had an outburst. However, for the most part, it was him and Antonio Banderas Jesus sitting by the fire with that giant book on The Boy's lap. There was even a time when he opened that book. It was a scrapbook of The Boy. Pictures of his life with cutout captions.

April 24, 2017 – Monday

The Zombie wakes on a plastic-wrapped mattress. He lies on the floor of a solitary confinement room. This is where they keep patients who are a danger to themselves or others. The four corners and floor are grey, cold, and no bigger than a closet. It reminds him of the closet from grade school where he spent his recess reading. He stretches out and moans in emotional pain.

A gentle male voice says, "It'll pass in time."

The Zombie turns his head to see a man (henceforth called The Dude) with a well-kept beard, short reddish hair, a round face, and glasses. He is sitting in a chair watching over The Zombie.

The Zombie remembers waking a few times and seeing The Dude outside the door. The Zombie rests his head on his arm and stares at the wristband they gave him upon entry. It reads, "Patient 013045-1," his name, and date of birth.

"It does," says The Dude. "I know it feels like it won't now, but with time it goes away." The Dude is warm and sincere.

The Zombie groans and replies, "No it doesn't."

"It does." The Dude leans forward. "When my dad died, I was a wreck, homeless, and lost. I never thought I'd be whole again. Then I found friends who helped me and over time it's gotten better. I still miss him, but the pain is fading more every day."

"This isn't a death." The Zombie does his best to avoid being a jerk. "I'm not trying to devalue what you're saying, but a death is different than the person you love, the person you'd give your life for, completely rejecting you and telling you 'you're a piece of garbage and all of this is your fault.' Death would be easier."

The Dude sits back. He spends a moment in thoughtful contemplation then says, "I've been there before as well. I had a fiancé. I loved…" He pauses a moment. Redness fills his eyes and he shakes his head. "I still love him, but he left me for someone else. Said many of the same things."

"And did you survive?"

"I'm trying to." The Dude begins to tell his story, how he managed, how he came to work for The Bin. The Zombie listens. Then it's time to get up and meet with The Psychiatrist.

The Dude leaves The Zombie to his privacy. In the corner is a small cardboard box containing all his belongings. He pulls clothing from the box and dresses, then meets The Dude outside the room.

They pass through the door to the solitary confinement room. It looks like a bank vault with a window. The Dude leads him to The Psychiatrist. Off of the great room, with the circular nurses' station, is a hallway with a number of offices. He is ushered into the first room.

The Psychiatrist is a pleasant Indian man who greets The Zombie with a warm handshake and a chair across a generic desk. It's a little hard to understand his accent but The Zombie can follow the questions.

They are the same questions from the interview yesterday. The Zombie must relive the same story of what landed him in this place. He is put on antidepressants with a slight anti-anxiety element. The Psychiatrist also suggests plenty of sleep because The Zombie is sleep deprived. He is prescribed an antidepressant to help him sleep and a sleeping drug to be taken before bed. Then The Zombie is patted on the back and sent out into the commons.

The days at The Bin are structured. There's a tiny room with a sort of drive-up window where they hand out meds in the morning. A line of strangers wait. The Zombie won't look up to see who they are.

When it's his turn, he sits in a chair. There's a tall cabinet with small bins in the back, charts lined on top of a counter, and cabinets hanging from the ceiling. The pharmacist on duty asks the same questions they will ask every day. "Your name?"

The Zombie plops his arm on the small counter in front of the window. He tells them his name.

"Date of birth."

The Zombie recites it.

The Pharmacist begins to plug away at a monitor and keyboard next to the cabinet, closest to the window. "And do you have any plans to hurt yourself or others today?"

Not really knowing how this goes, The Zombie replies with his usual brutal honesty. "I want to die."

The Pharmacist leans onto the counter so she can make eye contact with him. "Can you make a contract of safety with me?"

"What?" The Zombie shakes his head.

"A promise that you won't harm yourself."

"I promise." He honestly can't think of a way he could while locked up in here.

"OK." The Pharmacist returns to the computer, plugs away at a keyboard, there's a buzz and a click then two tiny drawers pop open on the cabinet. She pulls a bubble-packed pill out of each one, opens them with her nail, drops them in a tiny blue plastic cup, then slides a matching blue cup next to it.

Without a question, The Zombie lifts the pills up to his mouth. He hesitates for a moment. He has been down this path before. It leads to nausea, dizziness, self-hatred, and the feeling of absolute worthlessness. It comes with the admittance that he is a failure, a loser, and not normal. In his mind he says, *Screw it. Hopefully it'll kill you.* Then he tosses the pills into his mouth and chugs the water.

He says, "Thank you," pats the countertop and lifts himself to his feet. He wonders how many pills it will take to lose himself.

There's nowhere he can go. He doesn't want to return to that solitary confinement prison. On the opposite wall from the drug drive-thru is a counter with chairs at it. He flops into one and puts his left arm on the counter. He closes his eyes.

Fear, deep and guttural, like a million bugs crawling beneath his skin, takes over his body. It's hard to exhale. His vision blurs. The thought of The Wife finding out that he is here mortifies him.

She's already been telling people he's crazy. The Henchmen, In-Laws, and police cruiser are proof of that. If she learns that he's in a loony bin for the mentally ill, she will have the perfect narrative. "See, my mentally disturbed husband is in a psych ward. You all heard how manic he's been lately. I'm lucky he didn't kill me." Because that's what the press tells us. Every gunman and tortured spouse is mentally ill.

The Zombie is handed a card by someone. It has his name on it, which he barely recognizes. It has his food allergies scribbled all over it, a long list. Then everyone lines up behind the heavy double doors. There's a buzz and click and the line shuffles into the cafeteria across the hall for breakfast about nine.

It's a normal enough cafeteria. At one end is a receiving line with sneeze guards. The room is filled with long tables with people seated in plastic chairs. In the center, against one wall, is a drink dispenser. It only has water and artificially sweetened drinks. They serve juices and caffeinated coffee in the morning, then the rest of the day it's decaf. The opposite wall is filled with windows and a door out to a gated patio.

The Zombie wonders why a suicide ward would have so much glass. He takes the end of the line. He knows he will be the most challenging because he is celiac. The servers will have to change their gloves. It gives The Zombie time to survey those already seated. They must be from one of the other two wings.

It's a scene out of a horror movie. There are people with wild dirty hair. They lean over their trays and murmur to themselves. One lady wears a helmet. Most of them are shaking. There's a lady with long black hair and pale-as-death skin who starts randomly yelling then stops. A guy stands to return his tray. His crotch is soaked and the chair he leaves behind has a pool of yellow dripping onto the floor.

For a moment The Zombie feels unsafe. Then he asks himself, *Why? What are you trying to protect? The life you tried to kill just two days before?* Safety washes over him in the form of hope that maybe one of these people will strangle him to death. Then it dawns on him that this is the image he fears The Wife is creating about him, and his heart bleeds.

The first group leaves before the people from The Zombie's wing begin to sit. They all choose tables as far away from the wet chair dripping yellow. The Zombie makes no attempt to push away his anxieties to socialize. He doesn't care anymore. He's tired of fighting the worry that comes with every social interaction. He finds some empty corner and eats.

They're there for a half hour or so then return to the main wing. About fifteen minutes pass then a floor nurse yells that it's outside break. The Zombie doesn't want to venture out into the cold, so he lets them go without him. He finds a chair, hangs his head, and hyperventilates.

After outside time, they all meet in a sunroom at the end of the great room. It is filled with two long tables and a couple of round ones. A puzzle is spread out on one of the long ones. There is a fridge, counters, and a sink on one wall. The rest are all windows looking out into a metal-barred yard.

Again, The Zombie wonders about all the glass and how easy it would be just to slam his head through it and drive his neck into the jagged pieces that remain. He doesn't want to be here. The Nurses hand out check-in sheets.

The papers have questions about what he is going to do that day, feelings rated from 1–10, and a list of mental symptoms he is supposed to circle indicating how he feels. The pages will change slightly each day. On the back is the evening's check-in.

The Head Nurse stands up front and introduces the staff. Nearly all of them have a BS in *Psycho*logy with other degrees in pharmacy and medical. They do some motivational speaking and the patients are dismissed.

The Zombie still doesn't have a room and the closet he stayed in scares him more than the people sitting around a Plexiglas encased television.

Group Psychotherapy is next on the docket. The Zombie is expecting a circle of people talking about their feelings like in television and the movies. It's nothing like that at all. Everyone is handed a folder with pockets. It contains a journal. They're only given golfer pencils for these sessions and check-ins.

The Psychotherapy is an hour lecture. It's annoying. There's a tall twig-shaped boy who can barely keep his eyes open, and he interrupts the lecture to slur some statements totally irrelevant to the subject matter. Today it's about Trump, Nazis, Fascism, birth control, he crescendos on Hitler.

The Psychotherapist, a weak and meek man, affirms and continues lecturing. There's something about this man that The Zombie doesn't like. First, the man wears clothing far too large for his body. He wears running shoes with oversized khakis. He's slouched forward with his arms curled in front like a t-rex. There's nothing about this man that seems like an authority.

The Zombie learns he is in the suicide wing, which explains the patients with bandages on their wrists. It turns out that overdoses are the weapon of choice for self-destruction. Most of the patients are hospitalized for whatever they took—whether they are diabetic and pushed themselves to a crash, or they popped a bottle and chugged.

Interestingly, when a person formulates a plan for suicide, whether by hanging, shooting, or overdose, he or she will always return to that method as a sort of perverted obsession. Most of the people in the suicide wing are on their second to sixth stay. Most of them will try to kill themselves the exact same way they did the first time.

The lecture only leaves The Zombie more discouraged. He finds it hard to sit still. When it finally ends, he begins pacing around the great room. He follows the green tile that circles the entire space. Every few feet there is a door into a bedroom.

His thoughts return to the past two weeks and everything he did wrong. He kicks himself for reacting poorly.

The next "activity" is art therapy. Everyone is herded into a side room that is key card locked and shared with the wing of crazies whose meals overlap theirs. The Zombie checks his chair before he sits. It's clean. He slips into it and no one tries to sit near him which is fine.

He is given some permanent markers and a picture to color. It's a stained-glass sticky. He tries to block out the world to escape it. Then the art therapist asks for song requests. Every single one is a heart-wrenching love song. It frustrates The Zombie. He wants to yell, "For goodness sake, put something else on!" But jerks his chin upward to the left and continues to color.

Voices mingle into incoherent conversations. The Doped-Up Kid is arguing with someone about abortion. The Zombie does his best to add them to the noise he tunes out, but then The Art Therapist begins going table to table asking questions. The primary question she asks is, "What makes you happy?"

To this, The Zombie knows the answer without a moment's contemplation. He pushes the thoughts deep inside and prays The Art Therapist doesn't have time to talk to him.

"Patient 013045-1, what makes you happy?"

He thuds his knuckles on his right jaw and drags them to his chin a couple of times while trying to ignore her.

She asks again.

He doesn't want to say. Just the thought is burning his eyes and making it impossible to exhale. Fear crawls under his skin. The last thing he wants is to cry in front of so many people, but his wounded heart is thumping faster than he can count.

"Patient 013045-1, what makes you happy?"

He can barely say the words, "Holding my wife in my arms." Snot and tears stream from his face. The Art Therapist hands him a tissue. He spends the rest of the session trying to keep his artwork dry.

When they are done with art therapy, it's about noon and everyone lines up behind the locked double doors to the cafeteria for lunch. They take thirty minutes to eat, and then go back to their wing. There's another outside break time, more Group Psychotherapy, then a one-on-one with a personal therapist.

The Zombie gets the brutally honest but cute therapist (The Genius). The Genius makes The Zombie tell her the entire story.

She asks, "Do you think those things she said about you are true?"

"I don't know." More wrenching sobs pour out of him. "Yes."

"OK, well I can see that was rough. We'll talk more tomorrow."

The Zombie shuffles out of the room. They finally assign him a room. His roommate is nice enough. He wrings his hands and paces a little too much, has peppered black hair, is probably in midlife, and wears track pants and a polo shirt. Their exchange is short. At this point all The Zombie wants is to shower. He goes to do so and steps into the bathroom.

The bathroom mirror is some plastic material made to reflect a distorted image. The tiling is extremely nice. It's an odd juxtaposition to everything else, which feels out of the box from a hospital furniture catalog.

He turns on the water and it piddles from a headless faucet onto the tiled floor. He stands there staring at the pipe, then he saunters to the nurses' station and asks why there is no showerhead. It turns out the room is designed for older people. The showerhead has a long hose, so they can sit while they wash themselves. The Nurse tiptoes around the idea of it being a hanging hazard.

He is given one and is told that he has about fifteen minutes to take a shower before they get suspicious. Finally, he climbs into the shower and is hit with cold water. He is clean, dressed, and handing the hose with showerhead to The Nurses before five minutes pass.

Then he returns to the room. On his left is a small drawer-less desk with a plastic chair. The bed is on a built-in frame with a mounted headboard. It's covered in those thin white hospital blankets. On the right side is a tall, double-door cabinet. In between is a curtain with chains connected to a track on top.

His bed is behind it. The layout is the same except he is closer to the heater and window facing the steel-fenced courtyard. The Zombie sits on the bed. It crackles because, underneath the sheets, it's covered in plastic. All his things sit in a box under the desk. His Bible rests on top.

He tries to breathe but can't. His attention is focused on that box. Thoughts of everything that has happened over the day, past few weeks, his life, overwhelm him. There's nothing to fight and there's nowhere to run. A panic attack hits him. He fishes out the Bible, hugs it to his chest then falls onto the bed.

Crying has become more regular and discomforting than it ever has in his life. He is alone, unloved, belongs nowhere. His body has broken down. The lump on his neck is trying to kill him but it doesn't have the balls to follow through. He wishes it would.

Dinner is around five. They shuffle to and from the cafeteria. The evening is supposed to be time to interact with fellow patients, but The Zombie can't sit still. He paces the entire wing following the line of green tile around the nurses' station. He does the math. One loop equals roughly 120–150 steps, if The Old Lady doesn't get in the way. It takes him about 80 loops for 10,000 steps. He counts them all.

With his head bowed, he begins to count each loop. One, two, three, and then thoughts of his worthlessness creep in and he walks faster. Fifteen, sixteen, seventeen, he's going through yet another divorce. Twenty, twenty-one, she said nearly everything The Ex did to justify her affair and divorce. Forty-four, forty-five, forty-six, the millions of bugs begin to crawl madly under his skin. It's getting hard for him to breathe. He can inhale but his body won't let him exhale. One hundred twelve and the ruminations continue. Every stupid thing he's ever done in his entire life punches him in the chest. The bugs wildly dig around underneath his skin. The scrapbook is emblazoned behind his eyes with every disapproving face.

At 242, he begins to think about his love for The Wife. Every good memory causes the bugs to bite, each one deeper and more painful than the one before. He can't breathe, rushes to his room, collapses, cries, faints, wakes up, cries, and digs his fingers into the back of his neck.

The Nurses force him to come out of his room for evening group meeting in the sunroom. They lecture them on wellness and hand him the evening check-in sheet. It's a lot like the morning one but covers how the day has been.

The Zombie fills out the paperwork as quickly as possible and then returns to shuffling around the wing. He's no longer counting. Eventually, a nurse stops him to give him his evening meds. He dutifully takes them, continues to waddle, thirty minutes pass and he feels as if he is going to fall asleep standing.

Here he is safe, forced to eat, with no control over his environment. He can't even shower without permission. Every fifteen minutes, they check on each patient. He has spent his entire life needing control over himself, his emotions, his reactions, his environment, to feel safe, but this place allows no control.

He climbs into bed, pulls over the covers, and falls asleep. Dreams play memories of The Wife like video clips. Some are when they were happy, some are of when they were sad, some are of him begging her to return. All of them are nightmares from which he cannot wake.

Actual Journal Entries While in The Bin

Night 2

I had a dream where my wife came here to visit me. It was bright. There was a window looking onto a meadow with white flowers. I was still in Isolation with the mattress on the floor. She lay next to me. She giggled and smiled. She glowed. I felt good, at home, at peace, and then she told me she no longer wanted to be with me. She went from warm and open to closed off and mean. The outside turned red. I woke up defeated, hopeless, and with a deep sadness.

I told the psychiatrist about the dream. He was surprised I was dreaming at all and doubled my depression and sleeping meds. I tried to tell him I needed more anti-anxiety meds. He didn't listen. All my life, the doctors never listen.

Night 3

I dreamed about going on a date with my wife. She was single and lived on a second or third level of an apartment. We had a good date. We were smiling and happy. We walked up to her apartment. The sky glowed orange. There was a feeling of goodness and calm. In her apartment, she introduced me to her daughter. I talked with her as she gave the infant a bath. She was agreeable. She wanted to work things out and be married again. I was excited. When I woke, the sadness washed back over me. Hopelessness gripped me. I got anxious again.

Night 4

My dreams were all over the place. They mostly revolved around my wife. They seemed to be obsessed with her wanting a child. In the dream, we had several arguments about reversing my vasectomy. We even had a *Handmaid's Tale* type of breeding with a strange guy. I'd honestly give her anything, even a child.

1. I don't know if I've had enough chances to fix what is wrong. I know I haven't.
2. I don't know how I will feel if she learns I am here but doesn't visit.
3. I don't know how I will feel if she learns I am here but does.

I can't believe how much I took her and our relationship for granted. God, I can't lose her, not now, not when I'm just now seeing with clearer vision.

April 27, 2017 – Thursday

The Zombie meets with The Psychiatrist and demands anxiety meds. Finally, The Psychiatrist gives The Zombie more anti-anxiety medication, which begins to take effect. His day is like all the rest. He paces the green mile, calls his parents in the morning, ruminates, grabs his pills at the drug drive-thru, eat breakfasts, goes to group therapy but is unable to sit until the end, paces, ruminates, eats lunch, showers, group therapy, he has a panic attack that forces him to huddle between two chairs.

Pet therapy begins around two. He watches from the horizon of the vinyl armrest as a poor gray hound with a harness and a license tagged to it is surrounded by strangers. It tucks its tail underneath itself, shivers, and pulls its ears back. It won't leave The Owner's side.

Seeing that gray hound, a dog bred to run, in a harness, having a panic attack around a bunch of suicidal patients, saddens The Zombie. No one asked the dog if it wanted to be a pet therapist.

The Owner exclaims, "She loves doing this."

Really, thinks The Zombie, *can you ask her that? Can she articulate to you how she feels? How she feels surrounded, ganged up on, put in a horribly uncomfortable situation, powerless to do anything? Can you imagine what it's like to be a dog who only wants to run but is told it can't?* He says none of this then thumps his chin with his knuckles and buries himself between the chairs.

He meets with The Genius, eats dinner, more pacing, some rest between the two chairs, evening check-ins, a call to The Parents, spends time talking to other patients, realizes he doesn't care for any of them, happy nighttime drugs, and bed. There are more nightmares.

What is Culturally Normal?

There are hundreds of different antidepressants with more created daily. It can take a lifetime of therapy and medical trial and error to pinpoint an anxiety disorder and how to treat it.

With physical symptoms, it's rather simple. A man goes into The Doctor and says, "Doc, my arm has been lopped off."

The Doctor scratches his chin as he replies, "Sure enough. I don't see an arm, just a bloody stub where one should be."

"Is there anything you can do?"

"Sure...we'll have to experiment with a number of procedures." The Doctor flips open The Patient's file and begins to chicken scratch all over it. "I've got this one drug that might be able to stop the pain, but you could lose muscular control around your right jaw."

The Patient is stunned. "But I'm bleeding out." He points to the floor. "Look, there's got to be at least a pint of blood from the time I sat down."

The Doctor apprehensively peers over his chart. He makes a strange hum of contemplation, even tilts his head like a curious beagle. "I'd venture to guess it's more of a liter."

"I don't care how much blood I've lost," cries The Patient. "I'm bleeding to death!"

"Whoa...whoa...whoa." The Doctor backs away and says, "You'll need to stay calm. There's a lot of trial and error we have to go through."

"Fine." The Patient surrenders to the tragedy of the situation. "How long will this take?"

"Well...it will take the meds at least two weeks to fully affect your system. Then after that we will test you again, see how you've responded to the drug, and either change your medication or increase your dosage."

"Two weeks!" The Patient drops his head in sorrow. He watches the drip, drip, drip of the blood from his stub to the pool on the floor. "All right...let's give it a shot."

The Doctor excitedly replies, "Fantastic!" He clicks his pen. "I've got a cocktail of drugs you'll have to begin as soon as possible. Just four...no five different drugs." He looks up to reassure The Patient. "You'll need to take these morning and night. If you feel any paralysis of your limbs, fingers, or toes, call us immediately. Expect headaches and nausea beyond anything you've imagined, but it should just last a week." He rips off the prescriptions and holds them out to The Patient.

The Patient, anxious and ambivalent, climbs off the table, takes the scripts from his doctor, slips a little on the pool of his own blood, and asks, "You're sure this will work?"

"No...not at all." The Doctor smiles and adds, "Oh and please let our office know the minute you have suicidal ideations or feel like you're going to die."

"I feel like that now."

"I know." The Doctor pats The Patient on the back. "It will pass with time."

Pills, Pills, and More Pills

As The Boy aged, he saw many therapists and tried many different medications. One outburst in college and he was put on an entirely new regimen of medication. It made him physically worse, he gained weight, and he felt like a Zombie.

The trial and error was exhausting. Every time he took the pills, it was as if a piece of his soul had been chipped away. Church would constantly talk about the end times, and he often fantasized about the world just ending. He was a Christian. Death didn't scare him. However, waking up and going out into the world, that terrified him.

Through the grace of God, after fifth grade he never struck another person in anger. It was almost an unspoken blessing from God. The Boy never wanted to hurt anyone again, and God fulfilled that wish.

April 28, 2017 – Friday

The Zombie tries to sleep in, but the dreams, and a burly man waking him at 6:00 a.m. to take his vitals, prevent him from doing so. Pacing and ruminating, he calls The Parents, talks to patients in line for lunch, talks to them at lunch, sits through Psychotherapy, feels like a pile of crap, climbs into his two chairs, sleeps, wakes up for lunch, talks to more patients, goes to outside break.

It's a pretty day and nearly everyone is there. There's a patio with picnic tables. It's covered, much like the one he proposed to The Wife under all those years ago. He hides underneath it to stay out of the sun because he is not ready to expose himself to it. He and the girl with an Angry Face are both pale enough to fear the sun. She has a book, it doesn't register what book. He says, "I'm assuming you're a reader?"

"Big time." She's obviously nervous. The Zombie doesn't blame her. He has been pacing, panicking, and rocking in a fetal position for the past week.

"I like to read too. What are your favorite books?"

"So many." She looks up at him for a moment and then begins a list, many of which he has read. It's surprising because he has odd taste in literature.

He asks, "Have you ever read Christopher Moore?"

"Oh my God yes!" She steps closer to him. They talk about books for a while. It's not often The Zombie finds people who read, let alone the same books as him.

Outside time is over, he returns to pacing, ruminating, and group therapy. He manages to stay until the end. The Genius gives him several thought journal exercises to do over the weekend.

He leaves her and sits with the patients. They talk. He listens. They all go to dinner. He socializes. When they come back they decide to play a game of Euchre. The Angry Faced Girl becomes The Fellow Reader and is on his team. They goof off the entire time and he laughs.

Then it's evening check-ins, he calls his parents, socializes, takes the happy bedtime pills, and has more nightmares.

April 29, 2017 – Saturday

The morning phone call to his parents causes The Zombie to have a panic attack. He curls into a ball and weeps in the corner of the sunroom behind a dry erase board. The Fellow Reader checks on him. There's nothing she can do, but she is kind. Surprisingly he recovers from the attack and returns to his pacing.

The day goes on as normal. Then after lunch The Fellow Reader gives him a hug and says goodbye. She's checking out and for some reason it's difficult for The Zombie to say goodbye. She writes down her number and gives him some pens she has swiped from The Nurses.

Her absence hits him hard, but he has also made friends with others. The Softball Player is cool. She's the first one he opens to and she instinctively puts her arm around him, which surprisingly stops the oncoming storm that is a panic attack.

The rest of the day pans out normally. The nightmares are just as vivid as ever.

April 30, 2017 – Sunday

Sundays there are longer visiting times for families. None of his family is nearby. His parents are still in the Philippines. In the evening, The Good Friend, who told him to come to The Bin, visits. It's always encouraging to see her. She had been visiting throughout the week, but his mind never registered it.

She tells him that The Wife knows he is in The Bin. It throws The Zombie into his biggest panic attack yet. The Nurses rush him and The Good Friend into another room so as not to disrupt the other patients.

He sits in the center of the floor and openly weeps, inconsolable. A nurse is assigned to only him. She stays nearby and asks what she can do. His first request is to move to a room that has a real showerhead.

The Good Friend knows The Zombie is suicidal even though he doesn't articulate it. In one of his fainting fits, she digs the pen out of his pocket and has The Nurses go through the room. He had been trying to write with that obnoxious golf pencil all this time and the pens were a relief, but The Good Friend fears for his safety.

The visit ends with him pathetically saying bye to The Good Friend and assuming his position between the chairs. He cries until he falls asleep. He sleeps through evening check-in, and at one point he opens his eyes long enough to watch them move his things into a new room.

Then a nice nurse wakes him and gives him the happy sleepy time pills.
He takes them and curls back up in the chair.

Sometime in January 2003

The Boy, in his early twenties, climbed into the front row of the first day of a college course in communication. The room was a horseshoe with a blackboard stranded in the center. Somewhere, he had read or heard that students who sit in the front row score ten percent higher on exams than those who do not. So he does for every class.

The very short and assuredly Korean professor scurried into the classroom, dropped his suitcase on his desk, and grabbed some chalk. He introduced himself then turned his back to the class and drew on the blackboard. It was a nearly perfect yin-yang.

He stepped aside to give the class time to admire it. In heavily accented English he asked, "What is this?"

Hands raised.

He picked a boy in the middle row who answered, "The Chinese symbol for yin and yang."

The Professor nodded and asked, "What does it mean?"

It took the class a moment to catch up with the question. Then a hand shot up and a girl responded, "It's a symbol of dualities such as light and dark or good and bad? Balance?" She sounded unsure of herself.

"Yes." He pointed his chalk to the center wavy line in the middle. "And what does this line mean?"

No one had an answer.

The Professor, still pointing, asked, "No one?"

All were quiet.

The Professor waved his hand over the shaded part and said, "If this is the color of good," he moved the chalk to the unshaded side and asked, "and this bad? What are these two dots? What is this line?"

Again, no one ventured a guess.

"OK." The Professor sighed. "Duality, good versus bad. In each good thing, there's an eye of darkness. In every bad thing there is an eye of goodness. These are constant, unmoving. Sometimes they are parts of our character that will never change even though good or bad surround us."

He paused for dramatic effect then madly thumped the centerline and said, "The center is 'change.' It is essential and always flowing. Change is needed for balance. It is the hardest part about staying balanced. Change with the tides." He perked up and nodded yes as he continued, "Change is hard, but you have to change your thinking to learn both good and bad. Change keeps the constant," he pointed to the unfilled circle surrounded by white, "unwavering parts from moving, but it prevents us from being engulfed by one or the other."

May 1, 2017 – Monday

The Zombie ruminates about the night before and he can't believe any of this is happening. He circles the green tile. It usually keeps him from going over the emotional edge.

Today he is jerking his chin into the air. His hands are balled into fists and held near his face. Passing thoughts of the scrapbook flash into his head. A bully's hateful words. He slams his knuckles into his jaw.

The Ex telling him he is a deadbeat, another punch. Then The Wife's cold expression of disdain fills his imagination. He jerks his chin into the air. A nurse asks him if he is going to be OK.

He ignores her. The scrapbook pages flip faster and faster. His pace wavers outside the green lines. Red fills his vision. Water burns his eyes and his fists slam a puddle caught in his beard.

The Zombie staggers into the arms of a concerned nurse. She directs him to two chairs she's pulled together. He falls into them as spots of red are engulfed in complete darkness.

"Hey, buddy."

The Zombie's eyes flutter open and standing above him is his friend of sixteen years, The Bud. He's in a polo and khaki shorts. There's a look in his eyes. It's like the close-up scene in a horror movie when a victim sees the monster. It's a mix of terror and complete sadness.

A nurse brings him a seat and he sits next to The Zombie. The Bud's round face is contorted in a way The Zombie has ever seen. Normally, The Bud wears an unwavering smile, even in hard times.

The Bud asks, "How'ya doing?"

"I um…" The Zombie uses the armrest to sit upright. "I've been better."

The Bud scans the room with his small eyes. "This place doesn't look as bad as I thought."

"What do you mean."

He forces a chuckle. "I mean I was expecting people in straitjackets and helmets."

The Zombie crooks a smile. "That's a different wing."

The Bud laughs sincerely. It warms The Zombie to hear it. The Bud says, "I brought you this." He holds out a fidget cube, those palm-size boxes with switches, buttons, and dials.

"Thanks, man but you didn't have to."

"I know." The Bud swallows and looks down to his open palm. "I got one for my son and it's helped him."

"Thanks." The Zombie takes the cube and begins to smash the keys. They talk about how The Bud is doing. His family is building a house. The logistics are rough. There's a warmth and sincerity to him. He tip-toes around what has been going on in The Bin.

Suddenly, The Bud's happy countenance fades and he returns to that horror-stricken expression.

The Zombie asks, "What's the matter?"

"I don't know... I um..." He bows his head. "I never thought I'd see you like this." When he returns his attention, his eyes are wet.

"I never thought I'd be like this," says The Zombie in a halfhearted attempt to cheer up his friend.

Before long, the two hours are over, and The Bud says goodbye. The Zombie can't bring himself to climb out from between the two chairs. He watches The Bud leave.

The Bud

The Boy grew up distrusting everyone. He never had any real friends, so he didn't know how to handle The Bud. Around his senior year, The Boy gained new confidence. He wanted to break the cycle of never having a friend.

There was one funny guy in the leadership group. He had a round face and there was always a smile on it. He was funny and extroverted and he was a Christian. The Boy, with no experience at making friends, started bugging The One Funny Guy. He would hover around him and find opportunities to volunteer for the same activities.

The Boy would invite The Guy to things, and since he was a nice person, The Guy would say, "Sure." The Boy didn't really have anything to offer The Guy. However, the good nature of The Guy gave The Boy a chance for once. From that time on, The Guy became The Bud, his first friend.

Yes, there were summer friends he would hang out with at the campgrounds. There were homeschooled kids who shared the same circle as him. But he never had a person he could rely on, or reach out to for help, or help in return. The Bud was that guy.

In the context of friendship, all The Boy knew how to do was be loyal and stay in contact. He was there for The Bud's high school graduation. He was there when The Bud broke up with a girlfriend. Sometimes The Bud carried the weight of staying friends, other times it was The Boy.

Over the years, he was there for The Bud. The Ex hooked The Bud up with his future wife, her best friend. When The Bud married The Ex's best friend The Husband was in The Bud's wedding. He sat down with The Bud on his wedding day, with a plate of cheeses between them, and expressed the honor of being The Bud's friend, what a great guy The Bud was, and how excited he was for The Bud.

The Husband was there when The Bud bought a house. He did repairs. He flew back from Texas, and on a regular visit, removed all the carpet from The Bud's house to save his friend money. He was quick to visit The Bud when The Bud had a son. Again, he was there when The Bud had a daughter. He was there crying with The Bud when The Bud's mother was diagnosed with cancer. He retiled The Bud's bathroom. He did his best to include The Bud in his life and include himself in The Bud's.

The Bud reciprocated this friendship. He was there when The Ex broke The Husband's heart. He was there in The Husband's wedding to The Wife. When he needed someone, The Bud was always there. He was loyal. Time never changed that.

The thing The Husband hadn't learned was trust. He never really trusted The Ex. It came as no surprise to him that she had the affair. He also didn't trust The Bud with all the details. The Ex made The Bud choose sides and he chose The Husband. The Bud accepted The Wife and liked her.

There wasn't much to be said about why The Ex left The Husband. It churned up a dark time in his life when he was sexually and chemically self-destructive. The Husband didn't really see a point in talking about specifics. It would only harm The Bud's image of The Ex and paint a poor image of The Husband post-separation. He didn't really, truly, trust The Bud. How could he? He didn't know how. In a way, The Husband lied by omission to his oldest friend.

The Bud's unwritten rule about friendship was that there needed to be vulnerability between friends. The Husband faked it at times. Truthfully, he was only vulnerable to The Wife. So, in The Bin, when The Bud looked at him as if he were a monster in a horror movie, it shook The Husband. A new layer of guilt was slapped into the scrapbook.

May 2–5, 2017 – Tuesday through Friday

The week goes better than the week before. He paces less. His room has a showerhead. The nightmares wait for him every night. The Psychiatrist slowly increases the anti-anxiety drugs. There are fewer panic attacks. He is spending less time between two chairs and more time socializing. He works with The Genius on how to avoid self-destructive ruminating.

Friday, The Softball Player says goodbye. Even though he has made other friends, sadness washes over him as visit time rolls around and he watches wives visit husbands. Nearly a week of knowing where he is, and The Wife hasn't tried to reach out to him. This rocks him to the core. The dreams are the most anxious and depressing so far.

May 6, 2017 – Saturday

The Zombie gives in to the sadness. He refuses to get out of bed. They serve him his morning meds at his bedside. He dutifully takes them but refuses to leave for any reason. At lunch, a nurse wakes him.

She says, "Honey, you need to get out of bed and eat or we're going to take you to the hospital where they'll force you to eat."

He wonders why our society spends so much time trying to keep people alive who want to die. At first, he tries to completely ignore her as if she is trying to bluff him.

She adds, "Can we bring you some food?"

He ignores her, turns away, and falls back asleep while praying to God for death.

Moments later, The Head Chef wakes him. She's nice, motherly, and The Zombie takes a liking to her. She is usually in a hairnet but occasionally he catches her with her blonde hair tied up into a bun. He doesn't know how old she is, but she is older than him. She probably has her own kids and maybe an empty nest.

Her blue eyes sympathize with him as she says, "We have leftover breakfast, I've made some fresh chicken, and I made some apple cinnamon crumble gluten-free muffins for you. I need you to tell me if they taste good."

He can't look at her, so he turns to the bright sun bleeding through the shades of the window. "I don't want to eat."

"Sweetie, you can't go without food. You need to eat, not just for your health but because of your meds. Not eating will only make things worse."

Again, he is silent, playing chicken with their bluff.

The Head Chef places her hand on his shoulder. "Let me bring you some food. I don't want to see a good person like you sent to the hospital and have to start this all over again."

He looks up at her. She's honestly concerned about him. It's not even her job to be so concerned. That's the job of The Nurses. Here she is, taking time to do something out of her job description.

He sits up against the mounted headboard. "OK…the muffins sound great." He smiles real big. "Thank you. I appreciate you making them."

She delivers them herself.

He takes a bite and they're amazing. "I haven't had a muffin in years."

She smiles. "I'm glad you like them."

"Not just like. I love them. Thank you so much for making them." He takes another bite, and with a full mouth says, "You're amazing."

She pats his leg. "I'm glad you're staying."

He eats his meal, takes a shower, then steps back into the great room and paces the green tiles until dinner time. Then it's check-ins, more pacing, and nighttime sleepy pills.

May 8, 2017 – Monday

It is another day like any other. The Genius pulls The Zombie into her office. He sits in a chair beside her desk. As far as he knows, she is sitting in a wheeled chair in front of him. She says, "Patient 013045-1, can you please look at me."

He does. It is the first time he has honestly looked at her. She has long blondish hair, glasses, a cute nose and big eyes covered by glasses. She's attractive. It makes The Zombie feel a little silly because he has barely looked at her in almost two weeks.

In a deeply comforting way she asks, "What happened Saturday?"

"I wanted to die."

"Why? We've come so far."

"I know but…" His thoughts begin falling into something cognitive. "I can't live with myself. I can't live with the idea that I abused my wife. I can't forgive myself for that." He bows his head. "I deserve to die. I've been selfish and have a narcissistic personality disorder. I never wanted to be that person. It would be better for her if I was dead, then she could point to me and say, 'See he was crazy.'"

She reaches out, and with her fingertips, lifts his chin. She looks at him squarely and with deepest compassion says, "An abusive person doesn't talk like you. They don't want to kill themselves for the wrong they've committed. An abuser shows no empathy; they're narcissistic. They have affairs that dramatically pain spouses and then blame the spouse. They bring a person low enough to kill themselves. You're not an abuser. Just because you're a man, that doesn't automatically make you an abuser. Factually, we can prove forty percent of men are abused inside their relationships. An abused male is more likely to commit suicide."

A fire lights inside of The Zombie. The millions of bugs scurry out of his body. He realizes she has been saying this for days and it just now registers.

She gently lets go of his chin. "Yeah, in relationships we always hurt one another. Sometimes it's intentionally, sometimes it's not. We can be selfish human beings. Maybe there were times where you were abusive. You've got to forgive yourself, show some grace. You were willing to do anything for her, even die for her, and she still treated you horribly. You're too smart to think she hasn't at least been abusive over these past few months. Yeah, it's cumbersome to care for someone with your mental illnesses, but so is a spouse with a lost limb or one battling cancer."

She turns her attention to his chart in front of her. "Believe me, I've been doing this for a long time. Many people with narcissistic personality disorders walk through that door." She begins to write. "They are so self-consumed that they use suicide to get people's attention. They rarely see the reality of pain they cause others." With her hand on the pad, she turns her gaze to The Zombie and says, "Consider this—sometimes, in relationships, we reflect the illness of those we're with. You don't have a narcissistic personality disorder."

May 11, 2017 – Thursday

 T he days leading up to this moment were like all the rest. The one difference is the two echoes that manifest themselves whenever The Zombie prays or tries to ruminate. The first is a simple statement: "At such a time as this."

The second, "You've been given new life. Who are you going to be?" He thinks about them often. They harmonize with his last EMDR session where he was asked to comfort The Boy. He was asked to say something to the little version of himself to comfort him, but couldn't.

His parents move their flight forward by a little over two weeks. They arrive for the evening visit time. The Zombie stands at the edge of the wing. His parents are behind the locked double doors to the hall. He can see them in the window. They wave at him and he waves in return.

The Nurses beep them inside and The Dad rushes to The Zombie. They hug and cry. The Dad lets go of his son long enough to allow The Mom time with her child. They hug. It all feels surreal.

The Dad expresses that the top priority should be to remove the toxic thyroid as soon as possible. The Son gives him the names of the surgeons in Columbus within network. This information is conveniently on the back of the paper onto which he wrote everyone's numbers.

It's a fantastic moment, the beginning of hope. The Zombie is no longer completely alone. His parents still love and accept him. A still small voice says, "But I love you deeper, wider, without end." The Zombie ignores it.

May 14, 2017 – Sunday

The Parents visit for the extra-long Sunday morning family time. They go together to the specialized Psychotherapy. Then they meet with The Genius who explains to them the biochemistry of The Zombie's brain. How in those typical human fight or flight moments, much of their son's life, there has been so much energy, electricity, due to his disorder, that he could barely rationalize and process what was happening (she sounds all scientific and such).

It all makes sense to The Parents, just how much weight from their son's mental condition he lives with daily. They are thankful for the institution and The Genius. They appreciate The Therapist's wisdom.

After that, they attend music therapy in the sunroom. The day before, The Zombie started a puzzle, which he is intent on finishing. The three of them sit around the puzzle and chat as they put it together.

The Music Therapist passes around a book. Everyone is supposed to pick a song from it. She then plays the songs in the order given and everyone sings if they want.

When the book makes its way around to The Zombie, he picks out one for himself and one for his dad, putting his dad's first. The three sing the songs they know and continue to fit puzzle pieces into the Amish landscape.

Then The Music Therapist begins to play Gloria Gaynor's "I Will Survive." The Dad rocks out to it. He bobs his bald head, taps his feet while snapping, and he practically recites every word. She finishes, and The Dad asks his son, "Did you pick that one?"

The Zombie nods his head yes and replies, "For you." After all, his dad is a child of the 70s.

Then The Music Therapist starts the next song, "You Lift Me Up." The Zombie turns to his dad. Tears instantly well in The Dad's eyes and he buries his head in his arm.

In that moment, they both cry and sing. They reach out to The Mom and she comforts in her own way. While The Dad's life has opened him emotionally, The Mom has become a voice of wisdom. She is the rational mind these days.

The Dad says, "I hate music therapy. It makes me cry."

The three of them laugh despite their tears.

May 15, 2017 – Monday

The Parents visit The Zombie every night and tonight's no exception. That's an hour and a half drive back and forth just to see him for a couple of hours. It's a sunny day and they sit in the area just outside of the sunroom because it is far too hot.

While they are talking, a nurse comes by and hands The Zombie a slip of paper. It's a phone message. The Wife called. His ears begin to ring, and he sits back into the chair. His breathing is labored.

The Mom asks, "What is it? What's going on?"

"It's uh…" He bends forward onto his knees. "She called and wants me to call her back."

"Do it," exclaims The Dad. "We'll sit here with you."

"Let me um…" He points to the drive-thru pharmacy. "Let me take an emergency pill. It's supposed to stop a panic attack before it happens."

The Mom asks, "What?"

"Yeah, it's some anti-anxiety meds that I'm allowed to take as needed…I uh…haven't needed it in days…" The Zombie climbs out of the vinyl chair with the rubber armrest. He walks the length of the room, sixty steps, and sits at the counter.

The pharmacist asks, "What can I help you with?"

"Can I have one of the green and white pills?"

She pats the counter. "Sure. Let me check to see when you had one last." She pulls his chart from the shelf. "Wow…you're doing good. You haven't needed these in a few days." She asks him the same litany of questions.

He honestly replies, "No suicidal thoughts, no ideations."

She drops the pill in one blue cup and slides him another filled with water. He gladly downs them, hops out of the chair, walks thirty steps, grabs a phone off the nurses' counter, walks thirty more and plops into the chair across from his parents.

The Mom asks, "Did you take it?"

"Yep…" He holds up the phone and looks at the numbers. "Better living through chemistry. Give it about five or ten minutes then I can make the call." A panic attack starts revving up to tackle him. The blurs fill his sight, but then calmness washes over his head. He can think clearly, rationalize. He's in The Bin for goodness sake. What more can she do to him?

He calls.

She answers, "Hello." It feels like an eternity has passed from the last time he heard her voice.

"Hey, Bubby. How are you?"

"I'm OK…how are you?" There's a bite to her tone.

"I'm doing well. Much better." He can attest to it. The Psychiatrist has been increasing his anxiety meds throughout the week and he is having no trouble with social situations or general anxiety. The thyroid storms still hit him, but the green and white pills stop them from immobilizing him.

"I'm good."

"Yeah?" asks The Zombie. "Are your parents making sure you're eating?"

She feigns a chuckle. "Yeah. I'm eating."

"And you're making your own food?"

"Yeah. I think I've got the sweet potatoes and eggs down. Some of my dinners haven't been so good."

He gives an authentic laugh.

"So, what's it like there?"

"It's good for the most part." He tells her a little bit about the place and the food. How he has become addicted to the gluten-free bread. "How about you? How's work? Life?"

"I'm trying to stay busy. Honestly, the only person I trust anymore is my boss." She pauses for a moment then changes subject. "I've been seeing a counselor."

"Yeah?" The Zombie recalls all the endless prayers to God that things would work out, that He'd heal them. Hope makes him dizzy.

"Yeah…we've been talking a lot about your treatment over the past five years."

His heart begins to race. His vision fogs with red. Bugs crawl up his legs and he has to start walking the green mile. "What've you been talking about?" He thumps his jaw with his knuckles.

"Did you honestly think the things you did weren't abusive?" She continues with a list, "All the times you made me feel guilty for asking you to work. If I didn't do exactly what you wanted, then you'd outburst. You're so self-centered, so narcissistic, you argue your way out of every wrong thing you do and make me feel like crap. I've got no friends and your anxieties have imprisoned us to the house. We can't do anything social, so we just sit and watch TV all the time."

Instinct kicks in and shame washes over him. His reply is a knee-jerk. "I'm sorry. Please forgive me." He stops in the middle of the loop and grips his forehead. The bugs are causing friction, heat in between his muscles. The self-hate pours into him.

She huffs.

"Bubby…I'm sor—" The sound of that huff comes with an image of her cold disapproving glare. A panic attack swells inside of him. Blackness shrouds his vision and his footing staggers. He closes his eyes and breathes, just breathes. He can picture her, rolling her eyes, crossing her arms, and looking at him from under a condescendingly furrowed brow.

Everything he has done the past couple of weeks. How he was ready to kill himself for her. The entire household was run by her. She had control over all the money. If she didn't want to do something, whether it was go to the movies, or meet up with friends, they weren't allowed to do it. He'd feel guilty for doing anything outside of paying attention to her.

A still small voice says, "She's trying to shame you, guilt you, control you into doing something." Coolness climbs up his spine. The encroaching bugs digging at his legs scatter, leaving numbness that quickly fades. Blackness clears from his vision and the green and yellow tiles are the clearest they've ever appeared.

This has been her abuse for the past five years. Yes, he has abandonment issues, but she's been using them as a weapon. Every time he did something wrong, she corrected him through passive jabs, and withdrew her love from him. When that wasn't enough, she would make him feel horrible.

"You know what..." The Husband continues his trek around the room. "You're wrong. I'm a good person. I'm sorry for the times I've hurt you, but I was willing to do anything for you. I'm not narcissist or selfish." He chortles. "I've got half a dozen therapists telling me I've been the one being abused. I'm in the hospital because of you."

Then she growls, "Oh really? And you've told them everything?"

"Everything." The Husband shakes his head and finishes his loop.

She hisses, "Well they're wrong."

Again, he can't help but laugh at her. "And your counselor has heard the entire story?"

She's silent for a moment then asks, "So I'm guessing you don't want to talk dissolution? You take your half of the money and the things you brought to the marriage and I take my half and what I brought?"

There it is. He smacks himself in the head. The entire thing is a set-up to guilt him into giving her everything she wants. She barely spent any time searching him out over these past few weeks. She is ultimately responsible for her self-centered actions no matter what he did. "I'm sorry, Bubby, but if you want a divorce, we're going to have a divorce. I've been screwed over by a dissolution before, I'm not again."

She hangs up the phone.

He chuckles in disbelief and has to look at the face of the phone to make sure the call has ended. He finishes his stride back to his folks.

The intuitive Mom asks, "What did she want?"

"She uh…" He flips the phone over and bangs it on that side of the chair's rubber armrest. "She wanted to tell me I'm a monster… and uh…" He stops bouncing the phone. "That she wants a dissolution instead of a divorce."

The Dad says, "You said no, right?"

"I said no."

"Good," replies The Dad, "because you've got a lawyer, dude. You've got a lawyer."

The Mom looks pleased as well.

For some reason, The Zombie is not. There is something about the nature of ignorance that is blissful. It's hard to think this person he believed was amazing is the monster. It's hard to believe that he hoped to tell her he loved her before she hung up on him.

May 19, 2017 – Friday

The Zombie is released after eighteen days recovery from a program that usually lasts five to seven days. Today, he begins PHP (Partial Hospitalization Psychotherapy), which means he sleeps at home and spends his days in Dublin for Psychotherapy.

He walks into the room. All the chairs are lined in a semi-circle around a computer, a large-screen television, and a white board. He's thankful that the floor is carpeted and not tiled. People slowly fill each chair. As nine rolls around a new therapist enters the room.

He is nice, with a black beard, long matching hair, and a little grey that shows his age. He wears a button-up with vest and slacks. He looks like he has an appreciation for Native American culture. The few classmates who have had this therapist warmly greet him. The Man waves and introduces himself.

They begin by filling out a longer version of the check-ins at The Bin. Each person must go around and share what's on his or her sheet, as well as something about themselves, for the new attendees.

The Zombie can focus on the lessons. They are longer looks at different ways to approach stress, anxiety, and depression. They focus on how to proactively prepare for situations that may cause one to stumble back into suicidal ideations.

That same day he meets with a surgeon and schedules to have his right thyroid removed within a week. They will call him the day before with specific times.

Staying true to her nature as a rigid abuser, The Wife does everything in her power to passively attack The Zombie. She split bills and saddled him with late payments while he was in The Bin. They are still technically married. No dissolution or consented divorce has been agreed upon by The Lawyers. She is petty and mean.

May 24, 2017 – Wednesday

The Zombie is waiting on a phone call from his lawyer as well as the hospital for his surgery time. His phone, attached to her name and account, is shut off on his way to PHP.

He calmly walks through the long halls to the cafeteria. It has fake wood flooring, tables, trashcans, and a TV. There's a public phone he uses to call his parents. They're anxious about him not having his phone.

Then he calls the surgeon's office and leaves them a message to call his parents instead. PHP class begins, and patients aren't allowed to use phones during the day.

When the day ends, he begins the long drive back to Howard. Traffic slows him down. There is a pileup on the highway. It takes him an extra hour to make it home. As he drives up his parents' steep driveway, The Mom steps onto the front porch.

He climbs out of the tiny black sedan and says, "Hiya."

"You're safe!" The Mom sighs in relief.

"Yeah…what's going on?"

The Dad acts rushed as he bursts through the front door to the porch. "The sheriff was here. At first we thought it was bad news."

The Zombie stands next to the car. "But?"

The Dad says, "Your wife is trying to serve you papers."

Panic overwhelms him. He staggers and braces himself on the side of his hot car. His worst fear is happening. He wishes for a green and white pill to stop the oncoming storm.

They drive to The Lawyer's office and begin to talk options. The Lawyer is a handsome man, short, with a full head of hair. He is sharply dressed and oozes intelligence.

In the middle of the meeting, the sheriff walks in and hands the papers to The Zombie. He knows The Lawyer. They chat a little bit and then The Lawyer returns to finish his talk.

The Lawyer says, "Essentially, Ohio is a 'no-fault' state. Everything is cut down the middle. Because they don't have kids, it should be easy." Talking to The Zombie, he says, "All you want is half the equity in the house and the childhood belongings, books, and a couple wedding presents in the basement. That's agreeable. I'm sure that it should all be wrapped up by July."

The Zombie is physically rocking in his chair and plugging away at the fidget cube The Bud gave him. The red blurs his vision and he fights a panic storm.

The Lawyer continues, "Yes, she shouldn't have turned off the phone. It's petty on her part. She is the primary earner in the household, but because the phone is in her name, it's within her right to do so. Technically, you're still married, and that phone is shared property. You'll have to claim it in the settlement as an asset, but there's nothing stopping you from just changing the sim card."

A choir of gratitude erupts from The Parents and The Zombie. They say their goodbyes and climb into their red SUV. The Dad says, "You've got a freaking lawyer, dude!"

In the passenger seat, The Zombie grips the dashboard. Snotty tear-filled panic shakes his entire body. They stop to get him water. In the middle of drinking, another attack rams into him.

The Dad's voice trembles, "Do we need to take you home?"

"No," replies The Zombie. He composes himself long enough to walk into the cell phone shop, start his own line, and put the new sim card in the phone.

The rest of the night is filled with storms. He lies in his bed and stares at a corner in his bedroom. The basement is cold. He cries to God, "Why? Why are You doing this to me? Why do I have to lose her?"

May 25, 2017 – Friday

The surgery occurs first thing in the morning. There is a moment when The Zombie, wrapped in blankets identical to those in The Bin, looks at the monitors, all the cables he is hooked up to, the tiny curtain that acts as a fourth wall to his cramped room, and remembers his wife.

In December, The Wife was in a room just like this one. She was hooked up to all different machines. He remembers being lovingly by her side before and after the surgery. How her safety was all-consuming to him, how it was all he cared about. At this moment, when a husband needs his wife the most, she is actively trying to rid herself of him. She is actively hurting him.

The surgery goes well. The goiter is bigger than the surgeon thought it would be. They have to pry the clavicle to dig the goiter out of his neck. Other than that, there are no complications and he returns to PHP.

Somewhere in the middle of the week, during one of the discussions in Group Psychotherapy, The Zombie remembers his last EMDR session where he was asked to comfort that boy. Without the thyroid pumping extra adrenaline, without the fog of his anxiety and depressive illnesses, he learns what he would tell The Boy.

The question echoes through his brain, "At such a time as this, who are you going to be?"

To that he confidently proclaims, "I know what to tell him!"

The group therapy class turns to him and asks, "What the heck are you talking about?"

Spring 2000

The world did not end in darkness because of Y2K and The Boy attended a career center for his last two years of high school. He took drafting, not because he really cared about the subject, but because he liked wearing a shirt and tie every day instead of overalls and grease.

The bullying hadn't really changed over the five years of homeschooling. The junior year didn't feel any different than fifth grade. The only difference was that he worked hard to keep it from bothering him. He tried to manage the anxiety and depression with prayer and reading the Bible.

After a while, it wore him down. One day, the class was broken up into groups. Each group sat in a circle with drafting tables in between. Their leader was a girl The Boy kind of had a crush on, so he was anxious around her. He tried to pay attention and participate.

In his group, there was this Moon-Faced Boy, who was constantly picking on him. Just like grade school, The Boy was friendless, alone, and the bully had a tyranny of majority. The Boy also didn't want to be the baby who tattled, so throughout the year he had kept his mouth shut.

The specifics of what Moon-Faced Boy said have been lost with time, but every suggestion or effort The Boy made to contribute, Moon-

Faced Boy matched with a snarky cut which got the group laughing. The Boy gave up on the group and sat there, steaming, and quiet.

The conversation drifted to redesigning the front of a downtown restaurant and Moon-Faced Boy said, "Why don't you put this retard on it," nodding at The Boy. "I'm sure all that Italian food will do wonders for his bust size and motivate him to actually do some work."

The Boy yelled, "Enough!" He slammed his fist on the table and at the top of his lungs he screamed, "Shut the eff up!"

Silence fell on the entire class. Footsteps echoed off the hard floors, the painted cinderblock walls, and the twenty wooden drafting tables. The teacher, in his cargo slacks, perfectly tucked-in red shirt, and geometric print tie, grabbed the attention of everyone. Sternly, he whispered so all could still hear him, "What the heck?"

Shame washed over The Boy. He hadn't lost his temper like that in years. He could hardly believe himself. Every mortified face turned to expressions of "Oh look what you've done."

The Boy slowly turned to face The Good Teacher's disapproving glare. The Man's perfectly trimmed bearded face, dark skin, and brown eyes glared disapprovingly at him. When The Boy finally made full eye contact, The Good Teacher fiercely pointed toward his office and said, "Get in there!"

Murmurs swelled around him. One kid full gut-laughed and said, "Way to go, stupid."

The Boy yelled, "Shut the eff up, you fat horn dog."

181

"Now," cried The Good Teacher.

The Boy shuffled down the long row of tables, around a tall wooden desk, and into the office. The Good Teacher swung out the stool from underneath his own tilted drafting table and patted it. A mechanical project was beautifully, perfectly hand drawn on the table. The room was organized to near OCD perfection. Every book on the shelves was upright. The desk sat opposite of the table and a bay window. Pens were laid out perfectly parallel to one another. The Good Teacher swiveled the desk chair to face the stool.

The Boy bowed his head, and stared at his own brown suede, wing-tipped shoes and sat.

"Look at me," insisted The Good Teacher.

Shame told him to keep his head bowed but he resisted and looked up at The Good Teacher.

"What was that out there?" The Good Teacher motioned to the classroom.

The Boy shook his head. He didn't want to jump down another hole and dig deeper. "They were treating me like I was stupid. They called me fat and retarded."

The Good Teacher jutted out his chin as he asked, "Are you?"

It took The Boy a moment to respond, "No."

The Good Teacher disapprovingly huffed. "You aren't fat." He pointed to The Horn Dog through a window in his office. "That kid's fatter than you and he never gets picked on. You know what makes him different than you?" The Good Teacher grabbed the edge of his armrest and leaned toward The Boy.

The Boy shrugged.

The Good Teacher bent lower, so their eyes were at the same level. "The difference is that boy doesn't give a fly's rear about it. It affects you..." He pointed. "Because you care too much about it. If you don't want to be fat, and it matters to you," he spread his arms out and added, "then do something about it. Otherwise, take a lesson from that Horn Dog out there and accept yourself."

This didn't comfort The Boy even though he knew The Good Teacher was right. He rebutted, "Well they call me stupid."

"So?" The Good Teacher acted befuddled. "Are you?"

"I don't know."

The Good Teacher sat back in his chair and glared at The Boy. The chasm of silence seemed to stretch on for hours. He looked over his shoulder, through the window, then back at The Boy. He dropped his voice to a whisper, "When I was growing up, all I had…" he motioned to himself and leaned in so that their eyes met, "was my mother. I'd go to school and kids would call me the 'n' word. White boys like that knucklehead." He nodded to The Horn Dog.

"All that boy cares about is having sex. He's going to knock up one of those girls out there." He waves to the metaphorical outside behind The Boy. "He'll work some unrewarding job where he has to pay child support to three different baby mamas."

The Good Teacher opened his palm over his chest. "Now when they'd call me the 'n' word, I got angry, real angry. My friends and I got in fights with kids like The Horn Dog. Over one word." He held up his index finger. "One word. So, one day I decided to look up that word in the dictionary. You know what it said?"

The Boy shrugged.

The Good Teacher shoved his fingertips into his chest. "It meant ignorant, stupid, inferior. Me...as hard as I was working...stupid, ignorant, inferior...that was bull. After that, the word had no power over me. I grew up." He gripped the edge of his chair and bent forward again. "I moved on and became successful. I served our country in the Navy. I've done good, smart things, I'm a teacher. I know for sure, I've never been ignorant, stupid, or inferior because of the color of my skin or my home life. I've never been because I never allowed myself to be even when they called me the 'n' word. You get me?"

The Boy nodded yes.

"You're a leader. I see you out there." He pointed out the window. "When you speak, people listen. More than one time, I've looked up from my work and you're talking to one person. Minutes later I'll look up and you'll have three people all around you." He held up three fingers and circled. "Then after that you've got half the class around you."

The Good Teacher pointed out to that group of kids. "There'll be people who hate you for that ability just like there are people who're going to hate me because of my skin. Their loss. And you're trying to be a Christian. Son, sometimes that's tougher than being black. It takes balls to live that life. I could never do it. I do believe in God and I love Him in my own way, but if you're going to go out there and wear Him on your sleeve then you better at least meet Him with faith."

It was the strangest moment The Boy had ever experienced. Up to this point, the only people who had believed in him were his parents. Here was this teacher who barely knew him, and believed in him, who saw potential in him. It was the first time a teacher, any teacher, had done this.

The Boy walked away changed. He spent his summer eating healthy and being active. He lost weight. The following fall, he applied to leadership groups, debate teams, and speech clubs. The Good Teacher became The Phenomenally Incredible Teacher. The Boy even ran for some candidacy in school. He made his first friend, The Bud.

July 6, 2017 – Thursday

The Husband wakes from another dream about his wife. They are much like the ones he had in The Bin. It's always him enjoying time spent with her, him begging her to come back, or him making more compromises to gain her love. Every morning he rolls onto his back, stares at his favorite corner, and tries to convince himself that it is a day worth living.

Today, the weight of driving to Columbus daily, all the therapy, all the self-help books, all the prayers, and all the dreams have him the most confused. He can't figure out why she hasn't just taken out a second mortgage and signed the divorce papers. To him, there must be some purpose. God has got to be in it for some reason. He prays, "God, I can't get out of this bed. Please promise me a miracle today. I mean a giant one. Something so great that I'm encouraged to live."

The day goes on as usual. He lifts weights, cleans up, and drives to Dublin for TMS (Transcranial Magnetic Stimulation). Twenty minutes later, with a throbbing headache, The Husband hops back into his car and drives home. Traffic is congested. It adds at least thirty minutes to his drive. He makes it home in time for dinner, logs onto his computer, and an email from his lawyer pops into the inbox. His heart is racing. After all, he prayed for a miracle.

He opens the email. It reads, to him, that the alimony has been denied, the medical claims are inconclusive, and the equity in the house he built for them is undecided. He frantically runs up the stairs, out the front door, to the yard where his dad is working in one of his dozen hostess gardens.

The Husband pulls the letter up on his phone. He tries to read it, but a panic attack hits him, just like when he was a kid. He throws himself into a mad rage.

The Dad says, "Slow down. I can't understand you."

"Here!" The Husband hands the phone to The Dad.

Then the rage, the anger he has kept at bay for months, overtakes him. He falls on his knees. The grass does little to absorb the impact. He balls his hands into fists, looks to the cloudy sky, and yells to God, "I prayed for a miracle and You gave me this!" Anger, in such a magnitude he hadn't felt in years, boils over him. The bugs rush back under his skin.

The Dad calmly says, "Chill. Let me call The Lawyer and get a better explanation of this."

Still on the cold ground, The Husband yells, "All I want is half of what we put into that house! I just need it to pay my bills! I need it to get me back and forth to Columbus!"

"I know..." The Dad heads to the front porch. "I know."

The Husband holds a fist to the sky and cries, "God, where's Your justice? Where's Your deliverance?" He slams his fist onto his chest. "I've walked through every door you've opened to me without question. I checked myself into The Bin, I'm on six different meds, and I'm barely keeping my head above water! All I want are my needs met! You said You could move mountains! This is only money!"

His voice gives and he slumps forward. He weeps. She is still working a well-paying job. He has done his best to keep his mouth shut about her affair. He hasn't tried to contact her. The last conversation they had was in The Bin. He is being tortured daily over the guilt and shame that this marriage is ending. She is walking free of any burden.

Through his sobs, The Husbands says, "You say all sin is equal… You say that her affair is no different than the times I yelled at her or was self-centered…I've begged for forgiveness. I've begged. Please, God…let me see the purpose in all of this…"

It takes him a moment to compose himself. He stands. It makes him feel light-headed. He wobbles to the front porch, through the screen door, and into the great room. The foyer is in the living room with a piano on one side, a couch on another, and a dining table separates the kitchen from the living room. The Dad is on the phone. The Mom hovers nearby.

The Dad pulls his phone away from his head, stares at it for a moment, and then sets it down. "Well it's not as bad as we thought."

"OK?" asks The Son.

"The Lawyer had a conversation with the magistrate herself. She said they just can't justify giving you alimony because you live with your parents."

The Mom sighs. "That's just stupid."

"I know," says The Dad, "but The Lawyer is going to file an injunction so that hopefully we can get some retroactive alimony to pay for the costs from this summer. Also, with the medical bills, either way, she must take half of them. The Lawyer thinks that, considering the liability on The Wife for not getting the surgery in December, there's a case for her to absorb most of them. That's unsure. As for the equity of the house, she is supposed to pay you half of that and it's The Lawyer's belief that your wife is looking into refinancing the house."

The Mom asks, "How does he know that?"

The Dad shrugs. "I don't know. Either way, our initial hearing is scheduled for the twentieth of August."

The Husband shakes his head. "What does that mean?"

"It means that the judge will tell our lawyers who is responsible for what." The Dad's tone is encouraging. "That's good news. The Lawyer is going to try and get her lawyer to settle before that date. It'd be in her best interest to do so."

The Husband says little through dinner and the rest of the evening. It all pains him. He doesn't want to drag this out as far as it has gone. He would have signed the dissolution, but it never felt right. He needs help.

From that day forward, every morning, when The Husband wakes up from the nightly haunting dreams of The Wife, he prays, "God, I'm going to kill myself today. Give me a reason not to."

July 26, 2017 – Wednesday

The parents are taking turns driving The Husband to TMS. Today, the responsibility rests on his mom. From the passenger seat, The Husband text messages The Bud, "What's going on? Are you OK? Are you done with me as a friend?"

There are four one-sided text messages from The Husband. The past few weeks, The Husband has felt cut off by all but one friend, The Bestie. The Bud matters to him. The Husband's phone beeps as they drive up to the TMS office.

The Bud replies, "Well, I guess I don't know what to say. Over the last few months I've learned things about you that have me wondering if I really ever knew you. Your wife has reached out to mine and they've gotten close. She's filled in some of the gaps you seem to have left out of your first marriage. I'm happy you're getting the mental help that you need, but I don't think you are the abused one here. I think you've lied to me for years and that I really wasn't ever truly considered a friend. I don't want to get into a he-said she-said argument, but seeing how things are, I don't think I can stay neutral on this situation. I need to concentrate on my other friendships."

This bashes The Husband hard. Not only is The Wife trying to ruin him financially, screw him over legally, she is going out of her way to poison the relationships he has. She's been working on this for months, probably while he was in The Bin praying to hear from her.

Chaos washes over him. He replies something to the effect of, "I'm sorry I wasn't completely truthful with you. I wasn't ready to say something that would diminish your opinion of my wife because I was praying, and still am praying, for reconciliation. I'm saddened that you didn't reach out to me and listen to my side of the story. Even still, if it turns into dragging the other person into a harmful he-said, she-said discussion, I'll pull away from the conversation. That's for a professional to handle. I know you're busy and if having a relationship with The Wife is helpful for your wife, then good. I'll pray for you because my wife has destroyed me. I love you, brother. Take care."

The Husband and The Mom enter the sterile baby blue waiting room of the TMS office. They call him back. He breathes, inhaling for a count of four, holds his breath for six, and slowly releases for a count of seven. A panic attack, worse than he has had in months, consumes him.

He walks into the mapping room. In the center is a singular baby blue sort of dentist chair. He climbs into it, reminds himself to breathe, and they begin to tape the paper straps to his head.

They get him situated. He is still breathing, trying to push back the coming attack.

Then The Nurse asks the questions, "Name and date of birth?" She straps his head to the rest.

He replies accordingly.

She lines up the warm magnet to the left side of his head. "And are you feeling suicidal today? Any plans of harming yourself?" In minutes she would begin the procedure—a magnet would hit his head with waves to deaden the depressive centers of his brain. It's a lot like having a woodpecker digging for grubs in his head.

The question sends waves across his body. He feels confined and begins to rock, which is difficult considering his fastened head. Wailing sobs follow. There's nothing he can do. His vision hazes red. He is powerless.

She asks the question again. "Are you suicidal?"

He cries, "Yes."

"Do you plan on hurting anyone?"

"No."

"Do you have a plan to hurt yourself?"

The Husband rips his head out of the harness, assumes the fetal position and rocks.

The Doctor steps inside the room. It's as if he has never seen a full-blown panic attack. He asks The Husband, "Do you have any plans?"

In the middle of his wailing, The Husband cries, "Yes!"

Murmurs between The Doctor and Nurse collate into one statement, "We need to either check him into a hospital or The Bin."

At Such a Time as This

The Book of Esther tells the story of Haman and King Xerxes. After the king's beloved wife dishonors him, he begins to search for a new wife. Esther is radiant to him. He is instantly taken by her and makes her his queen.

Haman's hatred for the Jews and his thirst for power motivate him to squirm into the king's good graces. There, he convinces the king to kill all the Jews and take their wealth. The king agrees. An edict is sent across the land, and soon the Jews will perish.

This greatly troubles Mordecai, a Jew and Esther's uncle. So much so, that he rips all his clothing, rolls around in ash, and cries. However, he is also proactive. He sends a letter to Esther that reads, "Look, Haman plans on killing us all. You're in a position of closeness to Xerxes, please do something."

Esther is conflicted. She replies, "All the king's servants and the people of the king's provinces know that if any man or woman goes to the king inside the inner court without being called, there's but one law—all alike are to be put to death. Only if the king holds out the golden scepter to someone, may that person live. I myself haven't been called to come in to the king for thirty days."

Mordecai understands but replies, "Don't think that in the king's palace you'll escape this threat any more than all the other Jews. For if you keep silent about your heritage, *at such a time as this*, relief and deliverance will still come for the Jews from someone else, but you and your father's family will perish. Who knows? Perhaps you have come to royal dignity *for just such a time as this*, to use your place of power to deliver the Jews."

Mordecai is saying that the Jews are going to escape and still be God's people. Maybe God is calling Esther to this moment, *at such a time as this*, to assist in delivering the Jews from peril.

Esther boldly goes to the king and requests time with him. It only grows his affections for her. He tells her, "Whatever you ask for, even if it's my entire wealth, I'll give it to you."

She replies, "Then please spare me and my people from Haman's plan to kill us all."

This distresses the king. He can't believe he didn't know Esther was a Jew. He can't believe he allowed Haman to send the edict. Not only does the king reverse the edict, he replaces Haman with Mordecai. Haman is hanged by his own gallows.

Esther, the Jews, they were all saved because she acted on the opportunity to make change. When Mordecai asked her who she was going to be, a martyr or savior, she chose to give it to God and do what was right. She saved her people because, at such a time as this, she chose who she was going to be.

July 26, 2017 – Wednesday, Moments After
The Husband's Breakdown in TMS

The Mom and The Husband sit in the lobby of The Bin. Its tall windows cast the heat of the setting sun. The smell of lemons pollutes the air. There's nothing good about it because he knows it's masking a far worse smell.

The Mother angrily says, "I can't believe they'd threaten to call the police."

"They're just doing their job," replies The Husband as he cracks his neck. "They had a very large man curl into a ball in their TMS chair and openly weep. Anyone would have worried."

"But honestly…have they never seen a panic attack before?"

The Husband shrugs. He can't believe he is here, in this lobby with the heavy double doors, the lockers on one side, and a counter on the other. He swore to himself he would never be in a place like this again. If his mental issues never get fixed, he will go quietly in the night. There won't be any warning signs, he won't tell anyone. It will be done and over before anyone is the wiser.

There is a buzz and click, then the double doors open. A nurse steps into the lobby. She calls his name and he follows her. They pass the room he was taken into only four months ago. Then they turn right, down another wing, and into a room identical to the one they just passed.

There's a singular chair that rocks, a black end table with the same ugly boxy lamp, a plastic chair from the cafeteria, and across from it, an identical chair. He sits in the rocking chair. The floor is the same pee vinyl tile with brown marbling.

The Nurse takes his temperature and blood pressure. His panic attacks have reduced in severity and regularity now that his right thyroid is no longer an issue. He is already much calmer and functioning "normally." He even cracks a few jokes to The Nurse.

She finishes and leaves him in the room alone. Mounted on the wall across from him is a television locked in a Plexiglas box. In the left-hand corner of the room is a camera, one of those bubbles that stick a few inches out of the wall.

He sits upright, puts one leg on top of the other, and tries not to fidget too much. Who knows who's watching? If they perceive him as manic, which he does not feel, they could use that as a reason to keep him there. Already, he is trying to recall the questions asked by every therapist over the past four months.

Then The Genius enters the room. It's the same Genius who worked with him while in The Bin. Her eye makeup behind cute glasses is just enough, and her bright red lipstick complements her. She's wearing a floral top with a long chain draped around her neck and matching slacks. Her glasses fit her face perfectly.

She smiles and sits across from him. "How are you?"

"I'm well." He keeps his eyes locked onto hers. "How are you?"

"I'm good. I'm good." She nods as she opens a file on her lap. "Busy."

"I imagine. I didn't know you had to interview new admits."

She leans her elbows on the chart. "Not often but in certain situations."

He signs to his own chest. "That's a cute blouse and necklace."

The compliment takes her off guard. She looks down at them. "Oh thanks." Then her attention shifts back to him. "Tell me. What happened at the doctor's office?"

He explains the text message then says, "It just sent me into a panic attack. It's really the first panic attack I've had in weeks."

"Yeah...that's good. And honestly, from the sounds of it, that'd be a distressing message. He didn't try to get your side of the story. You'd think with a friendship as old as yours, he'd show a little more grace."

"Right?" He wants to scoot forward, but maybe staying in the same position is better. "It just seems like she's trying to get as many people as she can onto her side. There's no reason why she had to reach out to The Bud's wife. She has plenty of friends. Why mess with mine?"

The Genius straightens. "I can't say officially, but yeah, I can see why you'd be suspicious of her motives especially considering everything she's put you through."

"Right?"

"So...how's everything else?"

"Great really. I started my own business, I'm writing again."

She begins taking notes. "That's good right, because you're a writer and weren't able to have that freedom in your relationships or mental health?"

"No, I wasn't." Then he begins the litany of things therapists like to know. "I'm still meeting with my therapist and am taking all my drugs as prescribed. I'm working out every morning. I go to yoga at least two times a week, which is a lot of work." He warmly chuckles. "I'm not strong enough of a woman for it."

She laughs and tries to adjust her already straight glasses. "It can be hard." She nods. "Good. And no suicidal ideations?"

None aside from the prayer he tells himself every morning. He replies, "Not often. They just caught me at a bad time."

She swipes her hand across the air. "But no plan?"

"Nope." Truthfully, when a suicidal person formulates a plan, when they visualize how it's going to happen, they fixate on it. In The Husband's case, it's hanging. When the suicidal ideations occur, he tries to find the easiest way to make it happen.

"Well good. You're sounding and looking well."

Her compliment makes him feel better. "Thank you."

She stands and thumbs behind her. "Let me check with The Nurse."

"OK." The Husband readjusts himself in the chair. He wonders if he smiled enough.

The Genius is only gone for a minute then returns to the room. "Well everything looks fine. You can go home." She smiles real big.

"Thank you." He stands, shakes her hand and she escorts him to the lobby.

The Mom is standing with her arms crossed. She doesn't look as angry as she did when he went into the room.

The Husband waves "bye" to The Genius. She returns it. Then The Mom and The Husband are out the glass doors and walking across the hot asphalt. The Husband says, "Thank goodness we got The Genius."

"Yeah." The Mother still sounds a little frustrated. "She told me you're completely different from the person who left The Bin. She was really encouraging."

"That's good."

"I still think this was a frustrating waste of time."

The Husband sighs. "Me too. At least I'm not being forced to stay."

July 28, 2017 – Friday

The Husband begins pacing the East Liverpool Salvation Army's basketball court. There are 140 steps in a complete circle. He prays, "I just don't know what to do anymore. I don't know what to think or feel. I love my wife, but she continues to hurt me. I'm angry but can't bring myself to hate her. Please give me direction."

His brother, The Pastor Bro, steps into the gym. He is in full Salvation Army uniform down to the blazer. He has filled out over the years but plans on losing the weight. There is always a cheerfulness about him these days. He went through rigorous training school, married, and has a toddler and twins. He has the knowledge and the wisdom of perseverance. "Want to go into the office and talk?"

"Yes please." The Husband bows his head and follows The Pastor Bro down a tiled hall and into a side office. The entrance has a cluttered secretary desk on one side and a cubicle for the social worker on the other. The next room is his office, with an oak desk, comfortable guest seats, and bookshelves of theology texts. His desk is littered with material.

They start with prayer. Then The Husband, like a man in a confessional booth, professes every sin he has committed in the five years of marriage. Every time he got angry, every time he let his illness hinder her and their relationship. All sins, big or small, that have haunted The

Husband for months, are laid out to The Pastor Bro.

The Pastor Bro folds his hands and sits upright in his chair. "Are you truly repentant?"

"I am. So much so."

"And you say you're willing to do whatever God calls you to do?"

The Husband rubs his fingers into the side of his head. "I believe I am, from The Bin to the pills, to keeping my head low."

The Pastor Bro lifts his hands out to his sides. "Then it's washed in the blood."

"But—"

"No buts." He holds up his index finger. "Either you believe in a God who loves and forgives you, or you do not."

The Husband bows his head. "I know."

"God is still working on your wife. He wants her repentance just as much as you do." He pauses to point at The Husband. "You don't know what He has in store for her or you. Trust in Him. Surrender to Him."

"I have been."

The Pastor Bro folds his hands again. "No, you haven't. You're not forgiving yourself therefore you don't trust God and His provisions."

"Then why?" The Husband leans his elbows onto his knees. "Why am I still in so much pain?"

The Pastor Bro half smiles and says, "If you wanted to come here and heal your sorrow, your pain, I can't and neither can God. Because your pain is a sign of how deep your love is. That should be rejoiced.

Christ didn't come to die for our sins, the Bible says He came because He loved us. He knew He was going to suffer. We suffer because we love. The fact that through everything—through her destroying your friendships, you financially, you physically—you're still willing to forgive her speaks volumes of your character. All that you've been through in your life and you're still looking for the good in people. You haven't hardened your heart. You still love God. That's amazing."

The Husband sheds tears. It's not what he wants to hear but he can't avoid the truth in it.

"These hands," The Pastor Bro holds them out and looks at them and says, "they heal the broken, ailments. Your heart isn't broken; it's the heart of Christ. Your capacity to love is a testimony. Trust God, He needs more hearts in His body, His kingdom, strong ones that understand His sorrow and still love as He does."

In that moment, The Husband realizes he trusted The Wife with his heart and she hurt it, but she hasn't broken it. He knows that the only one who can break his heart is himself.

The Pastor Bro says, "Pray. If you don't know what to say, pray for those words. You've both sinned. All couples do. It's what we do in response to those sins that defines us moving forward. Are you going to let yours be washed in the blood or hold tightly to them? Are you going to forgive or turn her actions into bitterness? Because if you want justice, I hate to tell you, that's God's responsibility not yours. He'll deal with her sins in His own time."

"I don't want justice." He thinks about it. "I just want to be her husband again."

"I know you do." The Pastor Bro rounds the desk. "But…maybe God has something greater in store. By the end of this, as long as you can confess to God that you're willing to do whatever He asked of you to reconcile the relationship, you can walk away confident. Don't let your pain lead to sin. Ask yourself who you are going to be and don't look back from that decision."

Years of hurt flip through the scrapbook of The Husband's life. Faces with their cold indifference, their prejudiced hatred, and two wives turning their backs on him are all among the pictures.

The cutout sayings that often accompany scrapbooks are echoes of words that have weighed in his mind for years. "You're not good enough. You're a loser. You're a thug. You're too sick. You'll never be anyone. You're abusive, narcissistic, oppressive, and controlling."

Each page is just another moment in The Husband's life. They are mile markers of his past where he spends too much of his time. In the dead center is a blank spread, completely white. In the top left-hand corner is a cutout quote that reads, "The slate is clean, you've been washed by Christ's blood. Who are you going to be?"

He knows the answer. The Pastor Bro looks him in the eyes, and out loud he echoes the words from the still small voice in The Husband's head.

August 22, 2017

The Husband sits on a hard wooden bench in the Knox County Court-house front hall. He is dressed in the suit he wore on his wedding day. A plum-colored dress shirt, white tie, and pants with matching blazer, which he hasn't been able to fit into for nearly five years. A Bible is firmly cradled in his arms.

His Pastor Brother is dressed in The Salvation Army uniform. He sits upright with Bible in hand. Every attempt to stop The Husband from ruminating, every joke The Pastor Bro makes, falls flat. There's no consoling The Husband.

The hall is a long room with the entrance at one end and stairs on the other. Two officers and a metal detector guard the entry. The wide wood detailing, the time-stained wainscoting, tall ceilings, and bus station floor tiles date the building.

The Husband's heart won't stop racing. He prays repeatedly, "God, fill me with Your Holy Spirit, You're my mind and my body. Heal The Wife and The Mother-In-Law."

Then they enter. The Wife wears a new dress, plum with a white belt, ironic. She carries herself with smug superiority. None of her attention drifts toward the brothers. Her mother is in tow.

The Mother-In-Law is dressed for the gym, capri sweat pants, and a workout shirt. Bitterness and anger fill her countenance, but that is normal for her.

Their lawyer follows them and directs them to the second floor. All three walk past the brothers, chins up, shoulders back, never faltering in their laser-focused gaze to the steps. The Husband's lawyer is in the middle of a case, which was scheduled before them.

Ten after nine, two ladies walk through the door. They are decked out in full Salvation Army uniforms. The Husband turns to The Pastor Bro and asks, "Are those the new Lieutenants?"

He looks up and replies, "Uh-huh." Glee fills his face. "You think they're here for you?"

"I called them last week, told them the court date and time... I didn't think...I didn't ask them to come here." They both stand and ready themselves to greet the two.

It's a warm introduction. The Eldest Lieutenant has tight black curls, which are pulled back by a clip. She consoles The Husband by saying, "Believe me. I understand the conviction to remain true to a marriage covenant. My husband was having affair after affair." She looks down for a moment. "I probably stayed with him longer than I should've." She returns her attention to The Husband. "You can't hold onto a covenant on your own. It takes three, you, God, and your wife."

Before anyone can add anything further, The Husband's Lawyer exits a side room. He sees the crowd and his eyes grow larger. "Let me get you a room." He's in a navy suit. It fits him well. His hair is that perfect thickness with hints of gray peeking around the black.

The Husband hands over a stack of photos. They are pictures of The Wife's text messages. Her own words disprove The Wife's claim that The Husband's health and his intentions to get surgery so close to the divorce were only an attempt to harm her. Her own words show her denial of his need for care.

The Lawyer thanks The Husband and leads the four of them into a side room. There they sit around a large table. Again, the ceilings are high. It's a rectangular room with worn and dirty teal carpet. One window is on the farthest end.

They share each other's testimony, and pray. They pray earnestly for the hearts of The Wife and Mother-In-Law. They pray for protection and that God wins the spiritual battle. They've been praying for an hour when The Lawyer returns to deliver the news of how the assets are to be split.

He sits at the long table opposite of The Husband. He encouragingly says, "Your wife's lawyer tried to claim that the hyperthyroidism was under control and careful observation. That after seeking an endocrinologist, you decided to try and handle the situation with a nutritionist."

"That's a lie," protests The Husband. "A nutritionist was first consulted, and they strongly encouraged me to see a specialist. I did, and the specialist strongly encouraged me to have surgery on the thyroid within weeks. They set a date and the endocrinologist made an appointment with the surgeon. I gave you those texts."

The Lawyer gently tugs on his right earlobe and says, "Then the paper trail will prove her wrong. Right now, we don't know when her affair began. She started working for The Foundation in October. It looks like neglect of care. She wanted a divorce before she had to absorb the medical debt of your preexisting condition. It'll make it difficult to argue she isn't responsible for medical bills incurred after the financial restraining order."

The Lawyer takes a deep breath then adds, "She has made it clear that she wants to keep the house. Her attorney tried to argue that because the house was bought under The Wife's name that it belonged solely to her. She claims you didn't sufficiently provide for the household so you should have no right to anything. Of course, I said that's not how it works. The judge agreed. You're entitled to that equity."

Coolness climbs The Husband's spine. "That's good. Even a small buyout of the house will help me."

"Exactly." The Lawyer lays the edge of his left palm onto the table. "I made the deal, that if they simply bought you out of half the equity of the house, you'll walk away with some of the items in the basement and wedding gifts, along with your medical debt."

"That's fine."

"Hopefully," he adds as he makes eye contact with everyone in the room, "she'll be smart and just take the deal. Otherwise we'll go before the judge, total up all the debt, split it in half, and then all the value of the house, split THAT in half, and force the sale of the house. If she waits until then, she has the most to lose."

The Husband turns to The Pastor Bro. "Let's hope it doesn't go that far."

"Either way," says The Lawyer, "we'll know everything come October twenty-fourth."

The Curly Haired Lieutenant exclaims, "Where were you when I was going through my divorce?"

The Lawyer grins, sits back in his chair, and replies, "Thanks but I'm just a defense attorney and I'm only doing this for him." He lifts himself from the table. "I'll keep you updated. God willing, she'll take a second mortgage and be done."

They all exchange goodbyes. A still small voice tells The Husband, "Because her heart is hardened, she'll drag this out to the bitter end." The Husband ignores it and hopes for marital reconciliation or a buyout.

The Pastor Bro gives The Husband a big hug and says, "She worships a god of titles and money. The Holy Spirit will prove to her hardened heart that those are empty gods."

August 25, 2017

The Lawyers make arrangements for The Husband to retrieve his things from the house. He spends the entire day in prayer preparing for 5:30 p.m. He's nervous about seeing The Wife and walking into their home.

At 5:15 p.m. he meets The Dad at a nearby parking lot. The Dad places his hands on The Husband's shoulders and they bow their heads together. They spend a moment in prayer asking that the spirits of evil not be in that place. They beg for God's protection, that they not be tempted to lash out in anger if there is a confrontation or provocation.

Still anxious, but strangely confident, they climb into their separate vehicles and head to the house. As the gray home with purple shutters comes into view, The Husband realizes all his belongings have been shoved in boxes and set on the driveway. This is not what The Wife was ordered to do. They were to allow him into the house.

The Husband rings the doorbell. He doesn't intend to barge in, but he tests the handle of the screen door to see if it is locked. It is. The Wife, with that cold indifferent glare that is now all but cemented into the image of the person he loves, comes to the screen and through it says, "All your things are in the driveway."

"OK, well we'll try and make sure everything is there. But I'm allowed to go through the house and look for anything I may have left behind."

She glares and nods OK.

The Dad and Husband start packing the SUV and the black mid-size sedan. Nearly everything appears to be there.

The Wife steps out of the house long enough to ask, "What's missing?"

"Um…" He tries to survey the mass. There are a few things The Mom asked for, namely his baby quilt and a bench she made them for Christmas one year. "The bench and my baby things."

"The baby things are there." She points to a box.

The Dad digs through it for a second and yells, "Yeah, it's here. We just need the bench."

Red flushes The Wife's face as she disappears inside the house.

Tempests of emotion slam into each other in his head. How can he be so stupid? For months he's been praying for just a phone call, one good conversation, a date, reconciliation, a hug, and here she is with that cold indifferent glare.

The Wife and Mother-In-Law do their best to drag out the bench. The Mother-In-Law is wheezing and snarling. Whether it's the fact that she has to drag a bench from a basement or seething anger, heat distorts the light around her.

It takes all The Husband's willpower to show no fear. He feels en-dangered. It's not just the anxieties. The medications have those sorted. There's something dark, maybe a spiritual force, around these two. It reminds him of the story of Beowulf. After the hero kills Grendel, he traverses a dark swamp and dives into a black pool where Grendel's mother lived. Her evil twisted the land around her.

The Dad and Son duo pack up the things from the driveway. The bugs jitter across The Husband's skin. Red spots his vision. He prays, "God, what do I do?"

While he is not one to believe that God openly talks aloud regularly, a new conviction washes over him and the bugs scurry. He asks The Dad, "You ready to go inside?"

"Sure, man." The Dad is the Rational Mind and doesn't fear these two. Whatever metaphysical darkness swirls around them, it does not matter to him. It can't hurt someone so grounded. The reality is that under Ohio law, The Husband has claim to half of everything in that house.

The Husband leads the way. He comes to the front door, his front door, and this time absentmindedly grabs the handle. It's locked. This kicks him in the chest. He looks down at it in disbelief.

The Mother-In-Law, now Grendel's Mom, steps to the door.

"I'm allowed do a walk-through," says The Husband.

The Dad flanks him.

The Wife comes into view, passes her mom, and unlocks the door. A scrolling marquee of her thoughts runs across her face so fast it's hard to read them. Asterisks are flashing all over her expression, twitching her upper lip and brow.

They enter the foyer made by the back of the couch and the antique dresser. The Husband begins to open drawers. The first one is filled with 9mm bullets. There's never been a gun in the house, but there appears to be one now, somewhere. His face feels warm and the red blurs his vision. He breathes, just breathes, as he moves from one drawer to the next.

All the pictures are of her and her friends. There are a couple with her and The Bud's wife. She's been busy making her connections. The next stop is the television and cabinet. He digs out his DVDs and video games. Everything he pulls out he hands to The Dad.

When he stands, he is confronted with the top of the mantel. It used to hold images and symbols of their marriage, now it is filled with empty decor and pictures of The Wife with family.

He moves to the hall. Grendel's Mom growls as they pass. The hall closet holds some pointless things, but he fills The Dad's arms with them. Down the hall, he hooks left into their bedroom. Again, all their pictures are gone. The decorations are pointless. She's bought a new comforter.

There is a plaque he grabs off a bedside end table. It's of a scripture verse. The Wife gave it to him for his twenty-ninth birthday. She grunts but doesn't say anything. It goes into the growing pile in The Dad's arms. He notices mace on the nightstand and an alert alarm above the bed.

The next room is his. The futon has been laid down with two pillows. Someone has been staying here. He opens all his old dresser drawers. There's a stranger's clothing inside them, but the bottom shelf has a bunch of his computer things. He piles them into The Dad's arms. There's a can of mace on the desk inside this room as well as an alarm.

The dining room, with the table too big for it, has nothing he is interested in. He goes into the kitchen and opens cabinets. Nothing is registering in his brain. He can't figure out why she has thousands of dollars of food packed onto every shelf.

He moves to the basement. The gym is clean and in order. There's a can of mace on a bench. Again, nothing he wants. He hooks right, around the steps, past the laundry machines, and into the storage room. It has been cleaned. There's a lot more space without his things there.

In the middle is one of two space heaters. He grabs it. He returns to the bottom of the steps. Grendel's Mom stands with her hands on her hips in the center of the gym between two weight racks.

The Wife is at the top of the stairs. It's the first time The Husband has gotten a look at her. Her arms are skinny, boney. Her face is sunken. Any kind of warmth she possessed naturally is gone. She's wearing his favorite pair of jeans and, even though they are size zero, they've gone from tight-fitting to baggy. She looks sickly. It breaks his heart.

"No," she proclaims from the top of the stairs. She's stern. "You aren't taking the heater."

"Yeah." The Husband begins to lug it up the stairs. "I live in a basement. I need it." The Wife backs into the dining room.

Grendel's Mom follows in tow and howls, "You're lucky we even let you into the house."

The Husband yells over his shoulder, "You had to, or you'd be in contempt of court."

Grendel's Mom is blocking The Dad from coming up the stairs. She begins to reply but he cuts her off by saying, "Look, nothing will come from bickering, if you have a problem, have your lawyer call ours."

When Grendel's Mom finally lets The Dad by, she slinks into the corner of the dining room. Now The Husband is angry. He has been walked over all summer long. She was poisoning the minds of his friends while he was in The Bin. She is trying to destroy him.

He holds the heater up to The Dad. "Do you think you can carry this?"

"Sure," he replies as he takes it from The Husband's hands.

Then, with no fog of anxiety, no anger or rage, he steps into the kitchen and packs the expensive mixer with attachments into its bowl.

"Are you serious," asks Grendel's Mom.

The Husband watches the exchange over his shoulder as he unplugs the mixer and lifts it off the counter.

Grendel's Mom and The Wife are standing in the threshold of the kitchen. Grendel's Mom continues, "Are you seriously going to let him take the mixer?"

The Wife steps forward and jams her index finger into her palm. "You're not taking the mixer!"

Neutrally he replies, "Yes I am." Then he heads toward them in an odd game of chicken without any thought that they may not let him pass. They part and allow him into the dining room.

"You don't need a mixer," says The Wife.

"Yeah I do…" With a strong even stride, he marches through the dining room and into the short hall.

From behind him he hears Grendel's Mom give a guttural bestial cackle. The Wife yells, "That was a wedding gift to us. You have no right to take it."

"Yeah I do." He tries to navigate between the couch and dresser.

"But it was a gift to us!"

The Husband sternly projects, "There is no 'us,'" and follows The Dad outside to the dirty sedan. The Husband opens the passenger door; all the things including the mixer and heater fit in the front seat.

The Husband rounds his car. From the corner of his eye, he can see two women with scrunched faces and hands on their hips. The Dad drives off first then The Husband follows.

By the time they make it to the end of the block, The Husband is fighting a panic attack. The fifteen-minute drive to his parents' house gives him ample time to break down and cry. First, his vision blurs red, and then he can no longer exhale. He grips the steering wheel. Through his water-filled eyes, he glances at the mixer.

Shame and guilt take control of his throat and he screams so he can inhale. He spends the entire drive wishing he had never stepped into that house. He hates himself for taking the mixer. It didn't feel like a victory. Not in the way he had hoped. All it did was open the wound of his bleeding heart.

The First Weekend after August 25 – The Husband
Is Alone on a Saturday

The thing about pain and grief, at least for The Husband, is that it quickly clouds emotional, mental, and spiritual progress. Despite the slate being washed clean and covered by the blood of Jesus, he still holds onto the pain. This causes him to forget, maybe ignore, who he is going to be.

It's late. He skipped his afternoon anxiety pills. The timer for his evening pills, which usually knock him out, is ignored. He digs through his closet in the childhood room with the Legos put on display. He finds the brown belt he tried to use nearly five months ago.

The pain is overwhelming. It's dizzying. He threads the buckle past the holes to make a loop, then trudges to the basement steps. The open layout ranch home is empty and dark. He walks to the door that leads into the garage. It's solid insulated aluminum.

He ties a tight knot on the end of the belt, opens the door to the garage, steps inside, and closes the door with the belt in the top jamb. The garage is hot and humid. It smells like dog pee, oil, and old garbage.

All the boxes he pulled from his house are stacked on one side. It contains books, childhood memories, the bench, and on top is the mixer. Tears build in his eyes. He blinks, and they fall.

"I can't go on anymore, not like this." He says, "I can't endure another day of pain. Lord please forgive me." Then he shoves his head into the loop, tightens it, and steps off the ledge of the step. The belt pulls. It constricts around his throat. It's harder to breathe. He is choking. Panic grips him as he struggles to plant his heels on the step.

He can't find it. The red covers his vision and begins to turn black. Something inside of him fights. Finally, heel meets step and he pulls himself to a stand. He loosens the loop, slips his head out, then bends over and places his hands on his knees. It takes a while for the blurs to fade from his eyes.

"This is going to happen," he tells himself, "tonight." Then he remembers the sleeping pills in his basket of prescription drugs. He stands upright and loses his footing for a second. Then he pushes his way inside, pulls the pills out of the cabinet, and finds one of those plastic church communion cups. He assembles a cocktail of pain meds, sleeping pills, and antidepressants to help put him to sleep. It's an overdose that won't kill him, but it will make it easier to pass out with the noose around his throat.

He fills a cup with water then returns to the counter. The pills sit next to the cup. It reminds him of the blue cups of water and pills from The Bin. It's ironic that every time it was a sort of ritual, much like communion. The body and the blood but in the form of antidepressants, anti-anxieties, and mood stabilizer pills.

He takes a deep breath, inhaling for a count of four, holding for six, and slowly releasing for a count of seven. Calm fills him. He searches for courage from the source he knows best, the mental shelf where he keeps the scrapbook of pain.

He pulls it out and it is massive, bigger than he has ever known it to be. As he tries to open it, he loses balance. He then sets it on his knee, but he still can't open it without toppling over, so he looks around the room.

It has been awhile. His library of read books is larger than it was in high school. There is still a lot of room. There aren't any books with his name printed on the spine.

The window looks out to the yard with the trees. They are larger than he remembers. It's fall. Brown, red, and orange leaves litter the green grass. It's a perfect fall night for a fire. Then he hears the crackling, smells the sweet smoky burning of wood, and turns his attention to the sandstone fireplace. A gorgeous fire roars inside it.

In front are the two leather Victorian chairs angled to face the flames. Their red has faded. They are dusty from years of being unused. He decides to sit. Carrying the heavy tome, he rounds the chair on the right and slides into the old leather.

He runs his hand across the cover of the scrapbook. There is a beautiful cursive font that reads, "The Husband." He inhales and exhales. This tome will remind him of why he is doing this. It will churn up all the pain he needs to find courage to end his life. His fingers trace the letters and then end on the edge of the front cover.

A voice interrupts him, "I was wondering when you'd finally have a seat."

The Husband looks up to his left. There sits Antonio Banderas Jesus. He wears flip-flops, long dark blue jeans, a grey hoodie, and a plum T-shirt poking out between a half-zipped sweatshirt. His long wavy locks are pulled back and a charcoal grey yarmulke is on His head. There are some Hebrew words written on the side. He is watching the fire. Its orange glow lights His face. His hands are buried in the pockets of his hoodie.

The Husband replies, "It's not been that long."

Without taking His attention away from the burning logs, Antonio Banderas Jesus says, "It's been awhile."

"I know I came to this place, to You, after The Ex left me."

"Did you?" Jesus purses His lips. "I don't remember, and I have a pretty good memory."

"I'm sure I did." Shame washes over The Husband.

Jesus shrugs. "If you did then why is your ex such a prominent image in that scrapbook on your lap?"

The Husband bows his head to focus on the massive tome. He asks, "Where are Your robes and sandals?"

"Dude, you live in Ohio…and you return to a perpetually cold fall day. Why would I stay in clothing designed for near-equator temperatures?"

The Husband nods. "Good point."

Sadness overcomes The Husband. He says, "The Wife threw a fit over me taking a mixer. She tried to screw me out of all the hard work I've done. All I've wanted to do is love and forgive her, to be her husband again, and she cares more about a stupid mixer than me. To top it off…she used the excuse that it was a gift to us in hopes of dissuading me from taking it. A freaking mixer and a heater over me."

Jesus huffs. "Is that all?"

The Husband turns his attention to Jesus, who is still watching the flames. "That's a little insensitive of you."

Jesus shrugs. "If you wanted a sensitive Jesus maybe you should have pictured a purple dinosaur or Ewan McGregor with a beard and long hair."

The Husband closes his eyes tightly.

"Are you actually trying to picture Me as one of them?"

"No," replies The Husband, "I'm trying to picture you as that afternoon TV judge."

"Judy? The one your dad watches all the time?" Jesus laughs.

The Husband reopens his eyes.

The Antonio Banderas Jesus is still the same. "Sorry, son. You wanted the hardcore fighter of justice and love from those action movies and that's what you've got."

The Husband turns his attention to the glowing coals of the fire. "I'm in so much pain."

"So am I."

They sit there, quietly for a bit, contemplatively. The Husband asks, "How do You cope with it?"

"I trust my Father."

"I trust You."

"Do you?" Jesus turns His gaze to the tome on The Husband's lap. "Then why do you still have that thing?"

"I can't forget."

"No...YOU can't..." Jesus tilts His head as He pulls His attention back to the fire.

"But?"

"But...you can forgive..."

"I try."

Jesus chuckles. "I'm sorry but that book would beg to differ."

"How many times do I forgive?"

Casually, without a gap for thought, Jesus says, "Seven times seventy."

"But what if they continue to hurt me?"

"Seven times seventy."

"What if they are toxic?"

"Seven times seventy."

"What if we just aren't good for each other?"

"Seven times seventy."

"What if they are actively trying to destroy me financially, emotion-ally, and physically?"

"Seven times seventy."

"What if I've forgiven them four hundred and ninety times yet they do these things," asks The Husband.

"You were able to keep track?" Jesus shakes His head. "I can't ever seem to keep count beyond one."

The Husband grips the sides of the book on his lap. "I can't seem to stop counting."

"Well then maybe," says Jesus, "you should get rid of that scrapbook."

"How?"

Jesus shrugs. "However you want."

"But they haven't asked for forgiveness."

Jesus slides His hands out of His pockets, twists His body toward The Husband, and rests both elbows on the edge of the red chair. "Do you honestly believe any of those people in that book will ever come to you and ask for forgiveness?"

The reality of the question churns more pain. It causes feelings of powerlessness. "I just…I just want justice."

"Tell Me… What'll that give you? I made you into a literature person. How many characters, archetypes are fulfilled when justice is met?"

Again, the truth. It twitches The Husband's chin upward to the left, but in short bursts. He thuds his knuckles to his jawline and drags them to his chin. "None."

"None." Jesus sits back in His chair. "I died for those people in your book just like I died for you. Every one of them will have to choose who they want to be. The question is, why does that book bring you so much more comfort than Me, than this place?" Jesus looks around the room and adds, "More than the books or the talent I called you to?

You've ignored your calling fifteen years for the benefit of two different wives. How's that worked out for you?"

"Not well," replies The Husband, "but I don't know why I focus on this stupid thing so much."

"Yes you do."

"Then tell me."

Jesus sighs. "Because you don't trust Me."

"I feel like I do."

"Really?" Jesus turns to The Husband. "Then why were you trying to kill yourself again?"

The Husband searches for a good excuse but can't find one. It takes him awhile to ask, "How?"

"Easy." Jesus nods toward the fire. "Take that book on your lap and toss it into the flames. Then, you remember The Boy, the one inside you who is still suffering?"

The Husband pictures himself as the chunky younger version. Embarrassment rots his gut. "I do."

"Maybe you should consider comforting him like you said you would."

"I don't know how."

Banderas rolls his eyes. "Yes you do."

The Husband knows Antonio Banderas Jesus is right. Then he bends around the red buttoned-back of his chair, into the gap between him and Jesus, to look at the shelf. He focuses on one scrapbook. It's only five years old and has "The Wife" scribbled on its binder. The Husband asks, "What do I do about that?"

Jesus leans out of his chair. His head nearly meets The Husband's. "You've heard that old philosopher's question, Can God create a rock so heavy He can't lift or move it?"

"Of course…" The Husband keeps his attention on his most beloved book on the shelf. "It's kind of a cliché question."

"Maybe." Jesus raises his left eyebrow. "But the answer is yes. He can't lift or move a hardened heart. There's hope for her yet, but because God loved you, her, and the people in that book on your lap, He gave you all the free will to love, trust, and accept Him. What's the value of those things received but unearned? It's as fleeting as the love and life of a puppy."

The Husband sits upright and watches the dancing flames on the logs. "What happens after I do this? After I throw this in the fire?"

"I don't know." Jesus returns His attention to the warm glow. "My first guess is that it'll burn. The question is; can you trust Me enough to do as I ask?"

"I can but—"

Jesus lifts His index finger in the air and interrupts, "Let me stop you there. Like I said, no one in that book is going to ask you for forgiveness. Any justice they experience will be meted out to them when they are raised from the dead on judgement day. With all that said, why do you continue to be hesitant of letting those memories go?"

The Husband hangs his head. Tears drip onto the cover. "I'm so tired of crying."

Jesus laughs. "So am I. Honestly, it's not a weakness but a strength."

"How?"

"I don't know. You'll just have to trust Me on this one. But again, you're changing the subject so you don't have to confront the issue. Why do you hang onto that stupid book? Why don't you focus on one of the many good books on your shelf? I can think of at least one you could spend a little more time reading and dozens more you could be writing."

The Husband is not really enjoying this interaction. "The reason why I can't throw it into that fire…" He turns his gaze to the burning logs. "Is because I can't forgive myself."

Jesus places His finger on His nose and points to The Husband.

The Husband stands and laboriously lifts the volume from his lap. He stops to lock eyes with The Antonio Banderas Jesus. "Will You be with me when I comfort The Boy?"

"Aaron Daniel Behr…" Jesus leans forward and looks up at The Husband. "You do realize I'm just a manifestation of your wise mind using reason, tradition, experience and scripture to balance your rational and emotional mind?"

"Well…" The Husband doesn't have a retort.

"Listen…you asked Me for healing from your anxiety and depression and I've done that. You've seen so many therapists over the years."

Jesus pauses for a second then says, "The reason you believe in Me, the reason anyone should love Me, is because I have suffered and continue to out of love. You've tried healing the pain in your heart your own way. Let Me have a shot at it."

The Husband huffs, "You could've just said no."

"Aaron…" Jesus reclines in His chair. "I'll be with you. Even though you may not see Me, I've never left you nor stopped talking to you. You've just ignored Me, this place, who you are. Remember, you serve a risen Lord who wants to live with you, always."

The Husband furrows his brow. It's a truth, a reality he's been hearing all summer, all his life, from his parents, his brothers, and his quiet times with the Lord. He is no longer ignoring it.

He tosses the book into the fireplace. Embers fly into the air and float to the top of the book. They sear spots into its cover. It takes the flames a moment to catch, but when it does, the sight is gorgeous. It reminds him of the Texas sunset filled with purples, pinks, dark blues, oranges, and reds. The flames coming off the book put on a show.

The Husband flops into his chair. He watches the sunset on the scrapbook of his pain. Then, without looking away, asks, "Why the yarmulke?"

"I'm Jewish," says Jesus, "I can't likely worship myself."

"But the—"

Jesus interrupts, "Let's not have a theological debate tonight. This has been draining enough."

The Husband concedes. "And the writing?"

Jesus taps the Hebrew lettering on the side of His yarmulke. "It reads, 'King of the Jews.' You're not the only one rejected by the people you love."

"True." The Husband nods his head. There is a moment of silence as they share the fire. Then The Husband asks, "How long will this pain last?"

"Until the day you can literally throw your arms around Me." Antonio Banderas Jesus has a sunrise smile on His face. "On that day I'll say, 'Come, My good and faithful servant. Cry no more.'"

The Husband opens his eyes. His hands are tightly gripping the side of the green countertop with grey marbling. He chugs the water, puts the antidepressants away, and tosses the rest. He says aloud, "I trust You."

A still small voice replies, "Don't ignore Me, or The Boy, any longer."

A Long Time before April 8, 2017

The Boy, head bowed, maybe five, maybe ten, sits surrounded by a fleet of people. The Principal, The Gym Teacher, The Snow-Haired Teacher, The Art Teacher, The Ex, The Wife, The Father-In-Law, The Mother-In-Law, The Henchmen, The Hurt/Confused Mom, The Overly Rational Dad, and behind them is a score of bullies who've lost their faces due to time. The Boy feels worthless, powerless, different, like a disease, he is suffering and can't express exactly how or why.

All of the voices coalesce into words that reinforce the way he sees himself, what he believes about himself. All he wants to do is run but he can't. They have surrounded him, ganged up on him, for what feels like a lifetime. This pain will never stop. This isolation feels like an eternity.

Then, all at once, everyone freezes. They are locked in time and quiet. The Boy, with a tear-soaked face, looks up to see a new person amongst the crowd. This man has a shaved head, stands at a sturdy 6'2", weighs 220 pounds, has a broad muscular physique, and a heavy brow. He kneels in front of The Boy and stretches out his arms.

The Boy jumps into a hug with this man. It is tight and deeply sincere. So many times, The Boy wished for a hug but never received it.

The Man whispers to The Boy, "I know all of this hurts now. You'll spend a lifetime hurting. People you love the most will hurt you. Someday you'll want to die because it hurts so badly. But I promise you, through it all, you will be a good man. You'll never lose sight of the goodness in your heart, although your greatest strength is where you'll be hurt the most. Through it all, you'll never be alone. God will always be there to love and hold you and will never abandon you. One day your parents will be as well. You aren't a monster, you aren't abnormal, you are a good person."

There is a moment where they both breathe, just breathe. Then The Man asks, "Who are you going to be?"

The Boy replies, "A good man." Then The Boy buries his head deeper into The Man's chest and sobs. The Man rubs the back of The Boy's head because he knows it brings him comfort, and The Boy is comforted.

Acknowledgments

First and foremost, I give all the glory to God. Without Him, The Boy would never have become The Husband. God's grace is abounding and He is faithful. He calls us by our name.

The following people deserve more gratitude than I could ever express:

Brad Pauquette, the editor, who believed in this book and me when I lacked the strength to do so. He earnestly prayed over the text and poured himself into the book as if he wrote it. He is truly a great man, reflection of Christ, and mentor.

Emily Hitchcock, who read the beginning of the project and the end. Who loved it and marked it in red. Her skills as a copy editor are unparalleled. Her spirit is a blessing.

Captain Jonathan Jackson, a God-fearing man who took the time to talk me through the rough waters of this past year. He stayed up late and poured the word into me. He taught me, by example, to live confidently in my testimony, to not be defined by it, but to let God define me.

Lieutenant Andrew Behr, my brother, spiritual counselor, and often the voice of reason. This guy taught me how to find my faith again. He called me out when I was being frustrating. His response has always been to remain faithful and trust in the Lord. I look up to him.

My parents, Dan and Coralee Behr. Despite our differences and disagreements, they have always exemplified love. To them, I will be eternally grateful. They have never stopped encouraging me to write.

Dillon Sprague, a true friend, brother, and biggest fan. Without his friendship, I may have not made it through the dark times.

To all of you, thank you.

There are always more people to thank, and I look forward to the day I can express that gratitude in person.

About the Author

Aaron Daniel Behr is a regular guy who enjoys weight lifting and his work as a nutritional counselor.

He has been broken, pieced back together, stitched up, and has lost his identity a few times. Along the way he connected with literature and writing. He is passionate about the transformative power of reading, and prays it will never lose a place in our world.

This is his first published book and it won't be his last. His short stories can be found alongside the work of other great writers in the anthologies *Triskaidekan* and *For the Road*.

Follow him on Facebook and Twitter @aarondanielbehr and visit his website: AaronDanielBehr.com

Aaron currently lives in Mount Vernon, Ohio.